JESUS, CONTINUED....

WHY THE SPIRIT INSIDE YOU IS
BETTER THAN JESUS BESIDE YOU

J. D. GREEAR
AND TREVIN WAX

*The Word
is Power
BRO. Rick
2017*

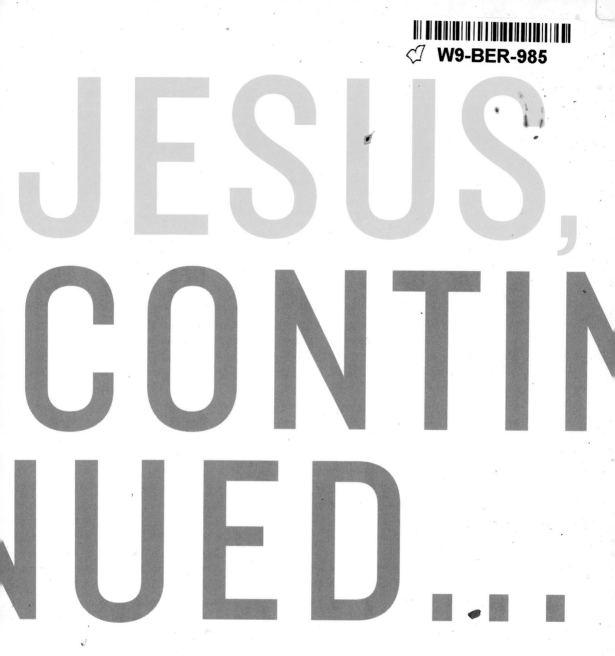

LifeWay Press®
Nashville, Tennessee

Published by LifeWay Press®
© 2015 J.D. Greear

ISBN 9781430042471
Item 005748699

Dewey decimal classification: 231.3
Subject headings: HOLY SPIRIT \ GOD \ BAPTISTS--DOCTRINES

To order additional copies of this resource, write to LifeWay Church Resources; One LifeWay Plaza; Nashville, TN 37234-0113; phone toll free (800) 458-2772; fax (615) 251-5933; e-mail orderentry@ lifeway.com; order online at lifeway.com; or visit the LifeWay Christian Store serving you.

Printed in the United States of America

Groups Ministry Publishing, LifeWay Resources, One LifeWay Plaza, Nashville, TN 37234-0152

CONTENTS

A LETTER FROM J.D.

For years I struggled to make sense of the Holy Spirit. What was He like? How could I know when He was speaking to me? What did His voice sound like? Some Christians seemed to obsess over Him, always "hearing" His voice in strange confluences of events or mysterious feelings. Others seemed to ignore Him altogether. They believed in Him, but related to Him in the same way I relate to my pituitary gland: I'm glad it is in there; I know it is essential for something; I wouldn't want to be without it; but don't really interact with it.

According to Jesus, however, the Holy Spirit would be to us, in many ways, what Jesus was to His disciples. According to Him, He is an indispensable part of the Christian experience. So indispensable, He said, that given the choice, we should choose the Spirit inside us over Jesus Himself beside us. That is a staggering promise.

This study is an attempt to discover the truth undergirding that promise. Through this study, you will learn how the Bible says the Holy Spirit speaks, how to experience His power, and how to follow Him faithfully when you don't feel or hear anything.

The Christian life is not a set of assignments to accomplish for God, but yielding yourself to Him so that He can do His work in and through you. In Him, God wants to give you victory over sin, and He has a special part of the mission just for you.

I am excited to see you get into this study, because I know that our Heavenly Father wants to draw you into His presence and fill you with His power. And I know that when members of a church operate in the power of the Spirit, they will turn their community—and their world—upside down.

For me, learning what it means to follow Jesus through the Holy Spirit revolutionized my walk with God. It transformed Christianity from a task list into a relationship. I pray that it does that for you, as well.

A LETTER FROM TREVIN

Bible studies fail if, when we close the book, we've grown in our knowledge *about* God but not in our knowledge *of* God.

Ever since I was a kid, I've been doing Bible studies—all kinds of studies, with all kinds of people, in all kinds of environments. The ones that I remember most are those that helped me study the Scriptures for myself, and in my study of the Scriptures, I encountered and experienced God.

I am praying that *Jesus, Continued* will be such an experience for you. I'm praying that, as you take this journey through the New Testament teaching of the Holy Spirit and His role in the believer's life, you will see His guiding hand in the past, rely on His power in the present, and be filled with His passion as you spread the news of King Jesus.

When it comes to the mighty rushing wind of God's gospel blowing through God's messengers and to all the nations of the world, Jesus says it's better that we be indwelled by the Spirit than for Jesus to be here physically present with us. We need the Spirit's power for this task.

The Spirit inside of us is better than Jesus beside us, J.D. Greear says. For now, that's true. But one day, it won't be one or the other. We'll be filled with the Spirit of God *and* face-to-face with the Savior who sent Him. I can't wait for that day.

Working on *Jesus, Continued* has deepened my gratitude for the Spirit's work in my life, and as to be expected when the Spirit is doing His job, it's a study that has increased my love for Jesus. I hope it does the same for you.

HOW TO USE THIS STUDY

Welcome to this 8-week study on the Holy Spirit. This study will lead you to understand what the Bible has to say about the Holy Spirit and what it's like to live in His presence and to experience His guidance. Here's how the study works:

INTRODUCTION: Each session begins with an overview of the weekly topic. Read this before your group meets so that you can better understand the topic and the context for your time together.

WARM UP: Begin your group time here with the discussion starter that is designed to help you ease into the study and to get everyone talking. Answer the questions that are provided and allow the group to dialogue about their personal study from the week before.

VIDEO TALKING POINTS: The video talking points serve as an outline of the main teaching points to help you follow along with J.D. They also serve as a reference point for further discussion.

GROUP BIBLE STUDY: The components of the group study reinforce J.D.'s teaching video. Read the focal passage, discuss the context, and then discuss the focal verse. The provided questions are designed to lead the group deeper into their understanding of the Holy Spirit as members apply what they're learning to their own lives.

PERSONAL STUDY: Five devotions are included for each session. These devotions allow group members to spend more time studying the Holy Spirit for themselves, enriching their Bible study experience.

JESUS, CONTINUED...

Jesus is still working today.

The Savior who cried "It is finished!" from the cross has purchased our salvation and accomplished the Father's will. His atoning work on our behalf is complete, but His mission to gather people from every tribe, tongue, and nation is going forward.

That's where we come in. Our service to God's kingdom is an extension of Jesus' works. It's something we do *with* Him, not just something we do *for* Him. Or better said, it's what He does through us.

At the beginning of the Book of Acts, Luke writes: "In my former book ... I wrote about all that Jesus began to do and to teach until the day he was taken up to heaven ..." (Acts 1:1, NIV). The "former book" to which Luke refers is his Gospel, in which he recorded all that Jesus did during His earthly incarnation. Luke says that these things were only what Jesus *began* to do and teach, however. The Book of Acts recounts what Jesus *continues* to do and teach—no longer through His incarnated body, but through His Spirit in the church.

In other words, it's not that *Jesus* worked while He was here and now the church works in His absence. *Jesus* worked then through His bodily incarnation, and He works now through His church. In other words, He is as much at work through you in your city now as He was then in the streets of Jerusalem.

As believers, we possess the same Holy Spirit that Jesus had while on earth. We have access to that *same* power; we are in communion with the *same* person! In this study, we hope to ignite your passion for the Holy Spirit—knowing His ways, discerning His voice, and joining His mission. We'll be looking at how Jesus continues His work today, through ordinary believers like you and me, filled with the all-powerful Spirit of God.

WHY "GOD IN US" IS BETTER

"How are you doing spiritually?" Now, there's a question likely to make you uncomfortable, and one that will probably elicit a "less than honest" response!

Your regular answer is "Everything's fine." You only missed your quiet time twice this week, pretty good considering your schedule. You prayed several times. You attended the worship service last weekend and served in the kids' ministry. You sent an encouraging email to a friend at church who suddenly lost a job. You had a spiritual conversation with a coworker who you hope to share the gospel with at some point.

But deep down, the question gnaws at you. Sure, you can check off your churchy behaviors, but something is missing. You did read your Bible this week, but you can't remember the last time you felt God actually speaking to you from His Word. You prayed this week, but it was like talking into the air. You went to church, but during the week, you lost your temper, gossiped, entertained lustful thoughts, and lied about something. So much for "everything's fine."

But what if the key to the question, "How are you doing spiritually?" isn't about what you are *doing* and more about the last word—*spiritually*? Emphasis on *spirit*. What if it's not that something is missing in your life, but Someone?

Feeling burned out? Disconnected from God? Unable to discern His voice? We've been there, too. And the good news is that God has a remedy for these problems—His gift of Himself in the Person of the Holy Spirit. That's why, in this study, we hope to show you how you can encounter the Holy Spirit in God's Word and in the gospel of Jesus Christ, and then how you can receive His guidance as you seek to join His work in the world and in your life.

WARM UP

DISCUSSION STARTER: The subtitle of the study says: "The Holy Spirit inside you is *better* than Jesus beside you."

How does this statement strike you? Right? Wrong? Surprising?

Why does this statement affect you in this way?

What do you think must be true of the Holy Spirit if the Spirit's presence *in* you is truly better than having Jesus Himself *beside* you physically?

VIDEO TALKING POINTS

VIEW SESSION 1 on the DVD and use the following bullet points as a guide.

- If you had the choice between Jesus beside you or the Spirit inside you, which would you choose?

- When you put Word and Spirit together, you get explosive Christianity.

- We desperately need a recovery of the Holy Spirit.

GROUP BIBLE STUDY

READ THE FOCAL PASSAGE: JOHN 16:4-15

DISCUSS THE CONTEXT

Jesus spoke these words on the night He was betrayed, while He was instructing His disciples in the hours before He would suffer and die for the sins of the world.

> What emotions do you think the disciples were feeling in this moment? What does Jesus say to encourage them?

Instead of encouraging them by telling them He would soon be raised from the dead, Jesus told them of the Spirit's coming.

> Why do you think He chose to comfort them with news about the Spirit's coming instead of His own resurrection or ascension? What does this tell us about the importance of the Spirit's work?

DISCUSS THE FOCAL VERSE

> [7] Nevertheless, I tell you the truth: it is to your advantage that I go away, for if I do not go away, the Helper will not come to you. But if I go, I will send him to you.
> **JOHN 16:7**

Take a look at different ways "to your advantage" can be translated:
"It is to your advantage that I go away" (ESV, NASB, NKJV).
"It is for your benefit that I go away" (HCSB).
"It is for your good that I am going away" (NIV).
"It is expedient for you that I go away" (KJV).
"It is better for you that I go away" (GNT).
"It is best for you that I go away" (NLT).

What thoughts and images do these different translations evoke as you consider Jesus' words?

As a group, make a list of all the activities Jesus attributes to the Holy Spirit in verses 8-15. Then, discuss how each one of these activities is "to the benefit" of the believer.

APPLY GOD'S WORD

What is the advantage of your relationship with the Holy Spirit?

Would you say your church is more likely to seek the Spirit apart from God's Word, or to read God's Word with little awareness of the Spirit? What are the dangers on either side?

What is the problem with thinking you can fulfill God's Word apart from the help of God's Spirit?

The Holy Spirit is described as "the Helper" in this passage. When you have sensed the Spirit's help? When have you sensed the Spirit's guidance in your life?

CLOSING PRAYER

Consider closing your group session by summarizing the discussion and then by praying this prayer of A. W. Tozer out loud as a group:

O God, I have tasted Your goodness, and it has both satisfied me and made me thirsty for more. I am painfully conscious of my need of further grace. I am ashamed of my lack of desire. O God, the Triune God, I want to want You; I long to be filled with longing; I thirst to be made more thirsty still. Show me Your glory ... so I may know You indeed. Begin in mercy a new work of love within me.[1]

Day 1
BEYOND ALL KNOWLEDGE
EPHESIANS 3:14-19

The Holy Spirit tends to be the forgotten member of the Trinity. Most Christians know He's there, but they are unclear about exactly what He does or how to interact with Him—or if that's even possible. Yet, as we discussed in our first group study, *something* was so important about the Holy Spirit that Jesus told His disciples it was to their advantage that He go away—if His departure meant the Spirit came (John 16:7). The Spirit's presence inside them, He said, would be better than even Himself beside them. In fact, they needed the Spirit's presence so much that Jesus told them not to raise a finger toward the Great Commission until that Spirit had arrived.

Forgetting the Holy Spirit affects how we view the Christian life. If we are unaware of the Spirit's presence and power in us, we are more likely to think of God as someone we know *about*, not someone we really *know*. In other words, we're likely to see God as more of a doctrine than a person. And that's when we stop expecting to feel God's presence in our lives. We stop expecting to interact with God personally. We stop expecting God to do mighty things in and through us, things we see Him doing through the early Christians in the Book of Acts.

> On a scale of 1-10, answer this question: Is Christianity more of a set of beliefs to which you adhere and a lifestyle to which you conform, or is it a dynamic relationship in which you walk with the Spirit and move in His power?

> | 1 | 2 | 3 | 4 | 5 | 6 | 7 | 8 | 9 | 10 |
> |---|---|---|---|---|---|---|---|---|----|
> *Beliefs & Lifestyle*   *Dynamic Relationship*

> Write about a time you felt like you were interacting with God personally, hearing Him speak clearly to you through His Word.

> Do you expect to sense the presence of God every day and hear Him speak to you? Why or why not?

Knowing *about* God isn't what changes your life. After all, James 2:19 says, "You believe that God is one; you do well. Even the demons believe—and shudder!" In other words, you can connect all your doctrinal dots and cross all your theological T's and still be no better than a demon. Knowing about God isn't what's central to Christianity.

Doing things for God isn't what changes your life either. Jesus warned that people will point to various "mighty works" on the Day of Judgment, works they performed in His name. And yet He will tell them to leave His presence, for He never *knew them* (Matt. 7:21-23).

Despite these clear warnings in Scripture, many of us persist in believing our Christian life can be summed up in what we know about God and what we do for Him. But we deceive ourselves. The Christian life isn't what we know about *God* and what we do *for* Him; it's about knowing God and what He does *through* us. This is love that goes beyond all knowledge. It's not just about filling our minds with theological truth, but having our whole beings filled with the God whom all our theology is pointing to!

Take a moment to read these words from the apostle Paul to the church in Ephesus:

> [14] For this reason I bow my knees before the Father, [15] from whom every family in heaven and on earth is named, [16] that according to the riches of his glory he may grant you to be strengthened with power through his Spirit in your inner being, [17] so that Christ may dwell in your hearts through faith—that you, being rooted and grounded in love, [18] may have strength to comprehend with all the saints what is the breadth and length and height and depth, [19] and to know the love of Christ that surpasses knowledge, that you may be filled with all the fullness of God.
>
> **EPHESIANS 3:14-19**

Summarize in your own words Paul's prayer for the Ephesian believers in Ephesus.

CLOSING PRAYER

Turn these words of Paul into a personal prayer to God for your own life as you begin this Bible study.

Day 2
THE PERSONAL SPIRIT
I JOHN 4:13

According to recent research, almost 60 percent of self-identified evangelicals believe the Holy Spirit is a force, not a personal being. Another 10 percent aren't sure. This means that 7 out of 10 evangelical Christians are either wrong or at least muddled about who the Holy Spirit is and what He does. It's also possible that many Christians who know the correct doctrine (that the Holy Spirit is a Person) still *act like* He is merely a force. Perhaps that's why so many "Bible-believing Christians" slip up and refer to the Spirit as an *it* rather than by the personal pronoun given to Him in Scripture—*He.*

Just before Jesus ascended to heaven, He told His disciples, "I will not leave you as orphans; I will come to you" (John 14:18). At the ascension, Jesus did not become an absentee God. He, as God, simply came to His disciples through a different Person. The mystery of the Trinity is that only one God exists in three Persons. Each person is distinct from the other two, but in experiencing one, you experience the one God who *is* them all. (If your mind feels as if it just exploded, that's OK. Christian theologians have been wrestling with that for centuries!)

In the same way that Jesus could tell His followers, "If you have seen Me, you have seen the Father," so it would be true for Him to say, "When you hear from the Spirit, you hear from Me" (see John 14:7). This Spirit, He said, would bring to their minds all that He had said and taught. In other words, He would make the Word of God come alive in their hearts, *applying* that Word to their questions and doubts. The Spirit would lead them through the Word, and they would gain the ability to obey that Word by His power.

Why do you think so many Christians find it easy to conceive of God the Father and God the Son as Persons, but find it difficult to conceive of God the Spirit in the same way? What hinders you from seeing the Spirit as a Person?

Jesus spoke of the Spirit as One who teaches us (John 14:26), and Paul warned against grieving Him (Eph. 4:30). How does considering the Spirit as a Person rather than a force make a difference in your attentiveness to His teaching or your desire to please Him?

Encountering the Spirit as a Person is vital to our Christian life. Why? Because the Spirit is the One who makes possible our life in Christ. His presence ensures that our Christian life is not merely a dutiful obedience to Christ's commands, but a delightful experience of Christ Himself.

Take a moment to meditate on the following verse from the apostle John:

> ¹³ **By this we know that we abide in him and he in us, because he has given us of his Spirit.**
> **I JOHN 4:13**

According to this verse, how can you know if you are abiding in Christ?

What role does the Spirit's activity play in providing evidence that you know God?

Stop and marvel at this truth for a moment: *God wants you.* He doesn't just want your obedience or acknowledgment. He wants *you.* He has always known you through and through, but now He wants you to know and experience *Him* so that you find in Him your greatest and most satisfying joy.

We'll return to this truth in greater detail next week, but for now, it's important to make sure we are thinking of the Spirit of God as a Person we *know*, not just a force we feel or a doctrine we learn. God has always desired a close, growing relationship with His people. He has always been a God who is close and present—but only since Jesus returned to heaven has He taken up residence *inside of us.* And that makes Him closer than ever.

CLOSING PRAYER

As you pray today, remind yourself that you are not simply speaking words but are interacting personally with the God who made you, the God who has saved you, and the God who now lives in you.

Day 3

SCARED OF THE SPIRIT
ROMANS 14:17

In some circles, talking too much about the Holy Spirit might cause people to question your doctrinal credentials. We're scared to go too deep in our experience of the Spirit's presence and power because we've seen other people go to extremes.

There are several reasons for caution. First, seeking an experience with the Spirit apart from God's Word leads people into dangerous territory. They listen for voices in their hearts or seek "signs" from God in the heavens. They always seem to be talking about what God "said to them" through a stirring in their spirit or in a strange confluence of circumstances. Their worship gatherings devolve into chaos, with strange experiences distracting from God's Word and His gospel.

In reaction to these unfortunate expressions, we rush to the other extreme. *We don't want to go there*, we think, and so we minimize any expectation of hearing from God's Spirit or experiencing Him at all.

> In your own experience, would you categorize your church as being more susceptible to seeking the Spirit apart from God's Word or seeking to obey God's Word apart from the Spirit? Why?

Secondly, another reason we may be scared of the Spirit is because He is controversial. Christians come to different conclusions regarding the gift of tongues, or the Spirit's baptism, or the Spirit's filling. Often you'll find that people in the same congregation differ on these questions. In order to keep controversy from breaking out in a church, the members keep quiet about the Spirit altogether. They think that affirming the basic truths about the Spirit is sufficient. Anything more may lead to disunity.

It's true that getting hung up on secondary questions can distract us from our mission. But avoiding the Spirit in order to avoid the secondary issues is another way of keeping us from experiencing His presence and power.

> When have you had a disagreement with another believer over a doctrinal matter? Under what circumstances are doctrinal debates helpful? Under what circumstances are they distracting?

There is a third reason why we may be scared of the Spirit, and this reason is more personal. Perhaps we are afraid of the Spirit *because of what He may ask of us*. We see how the Spirit worked in the early church, how He guided and empowered believers, and rather than be excited by such activity, we're frightened. We find it more comfortable to keep God at arm's length, to focus on our behavior rather than our hearts, to focus on Him doctrinally rather than experientially, *because we're afraid He will call us to step out of our comfort zones.*

> Out of the three reasons listed that we are often afraid of the Spirit's working, which one most resonates with you? Why?

In his letter to the Romans, the apostle Paul encouraged believers to avoid causing unnecessary offense to other believers. He spoke specifically about how Christians should avoid passing judgment on one another by what they eat and drink. But then, he described the kingdom of God in a unique way:

> [17] For the kingdom of God is not a matter of eating and drinking
> but of righteousness and peace and joy in the Holy Spirit.
> **ROMANS 14:17**

According to this verse, the kingdom of God is righteousness (Christ's righteousness given to us in salvation and the righteous behavior He is working in us), peace (with God and with others), and joy granted by the Holy Spirit. Too often, we associate the Spirit with crazy manifestations, division in the church, or fear of what He may ask of us.

But this verse flips our way of thinking upside down. The Spirit's presence doesn't lead to distracting and self-focused practices of piety, but the righteousness of God's kingdom. The Spirit's presence doesn't stir up division, but peace with God and with our brothers and sisters in Christ. The Spirit's presence doesn't grant us fear, but joy in fulfilling His will.

CLOSING PRAYER

Spend some time asking God to soften your heart and prepare you for experiencing the presence and power of His Spirit.

Day 4
THE NECESSARY SPIRIT
LUKE 24:49

What if we told you we've gotten the Great Commission all wrong? What if Jesus' instructions aren't first "go and tell" but "go and wait"? Perhaps we'd be overstating our case, but maybe not. Notice how Luke recounts the commissioning of the disciples, especially the last verse:

> [45] Then [Jesus] opened their minds to understand the Scriptures,
> [46] and He said to them, "Thus it is written, that the Christ would suffer
> and rise again from the dead the third day, [47] and that repentance for
> forgiveness of sins would be proclaimed in His name to all the nations,
> beginning from Jerusalem. [48] You are witnesses of these things. [49] And
> behold, I am sending forth the promise of My Father upon you; but you
> are to stay in the city until you are clothed with power from on high."
> **LUKE 24:45-49, NASB**

The fact that Jesus' command before His ascension is "go and wait" rather than "go and tell" underscores the importance of the Holy Spirit's role in enabling the disciples to live up to the identity Jesus has given them. What happens if we miss this point? We will overestimate the work we can do in our own power. And we will downplay the necessity of the Spirit in the work of taking the gospel to the nations.

Does the idea of taking the gospel to the ends of the earth invigorate you or exhaust you? Why?

Write about a time when you felt burned out or exhausted by the work you were doing for God while feeling disconnected from His presence and power. What factors played into this experience?

Christ's command to follow Him and to take His gospel to the ends of the earth is an obligation for every believer. But this is an obligation that comes with a gift. And this gift is a Person—the Holy Spirit, who was promised in the Old Testament.

Consider Ezekiel 36:

> [25] I will sprinkle clean water on you, and you shall be clean from all
> your uncleannesses, and from all your idols I will cleanse you.
> [26] And I will give you a new heart, and a new spirit I will put within
> you. And I will remove the heart of stone from your flesh and give
> you a heart of flesh. [27] And I will put my Spirit within you, and cause
> you to walk in my statutes and be careful to obey my rules.
> **EZEKIEL 36:25-27**

In the passage above, underline everything God promises to do for His people. Circle any reference to the Spirit.

Do you see how the gospel grants us not only forgiveness, but also the Spirit's presence? The promise of God in the Old Testament was that His people would be given new hearts and be empowered for ministry through the Person and work of the Spirit. Apart from supernatural intervention, the disciples were powerless to accomplish the task Jesus set before them.

Sometimes, we focus so much on methods and tools for sharing the gospel, funding mission work, and building up the church that we lose sight of an important truth: *Far more important than having a plan is relying on a Person.* Tools and methods are optional and interchangeable, but the Holy Spirit is absolutely necessary.

Our reliance on the Holy Spirit can be measured not by the number of books we read and strategies we implement, but by the time and energy we spend in prayer for the Spirit's power and work to be manifested in our lives. Relying on the Spirit does not negate the importance of planning, prioritizing, and strategizing (as is evident in the way the apostles made plans as they took the gospel to the nations), but it keeps methods and tools in proper perspective. What matters most is cultivating a holy desperation for the Spirit to accomplish God's will in and through us.

CLOSING PRAYER

Thank the Lord for fulfilling His promise to give you the Holy Spirit. Ask Him to reveal to you today your utter dependence on Him as you seek to fulfill His will.

Day 5
WORD AND SPIRIT
2 PETER 1:16-19

The vibrant Christian life is a union of clarity in the Word and openness to the Spirit. If we seek the Spirit of God apart from the Word of God, our faith will end in shipwreck. More havoc has been wreaked in the church following the words, "The Spirit of God just said to me ..." than any other phrase. God's Spirit *never* operates independently of His Word. Why would He?

But, in the same way, if you seek to obey the Word apart from the power of the Spirit, not only will your spiritual life be lifeless and dull, you'll also miss out on the help God wants to give you and the most exciting things He has planned for you. You'll miss out on the dynamism of *relationship*.

So, seek the Spirit in the Word. His guidance functions something like steering a bicycle: It works only once you're moving. The Spirit steers as you obey God's commands. You rely on His power to start pedaling in obedience, and then as you pedal, you watch Him start directing.

Or here's another way to think about it: The Spirit of God draws upon our knowledge of the Word of God to counsel and encourage us like a gunner draws upon a stash of ammunition. If no ammunition waits in the chamber, the gunner simply has nothing to work with. The most powerful gun with no ammunition is impotent.

If you want to be led by the Spirit of God, then devote yourself to the Word of God. When it comes to the voice of God, the Scriptures are in a class all by themselves. God is always speaking clearly and reliably there.

You won't know the Spirit any more than you know the Word. So if you want to walk with the Spirit of God, get on your knees and open your Bible.

Consider the state of your walk with God right now. What role does reading Scripture play in your spiritual life?

On the right, write down a list of Bible verses or passages you have memorized or know well enough that the Spirit could use to counsel and encourage you. On the left, write down a few passages of Scripture you'd like to memorize or know better, in order to have more "ammunition in the chamber."

Consider what the apostle Peter said about God's Word:

> ¹⁶ For we did not follow cleverly devised myths when we made known to you the power and coming of our Lord Jesus Christ, but we were eyewitnesses of his majesty. ¹⁷ For when he received honor and glory from God the Father, and the voice was borne to him by the Majestic Glory, "This is my beloved Son, with whom I am well pleased," ¹⁸ we ourselves heard this very voice borne from heaven, for we were with him on the holy mountain. ¹⁹ And we have the prophetic word more fully confirmed, to which you will do well to pay attention as to a lamp shining in a dark place, until the day dawns and the morning star rises in your hearts.
>
> **2 PETER 1:16-19**

Peter described the Scriptures as "the prophetic word more fully confirmed" than even the voice he heard at Jesus' baptism. How is your reading of the Bible impacted by knowing that Scripture is "more sure" than if you were to hear an audible voice from heaven?

Throughout the remainder of this study, we want to show you how God's Word and God's Spirit operate together in one powerful dynamic. While pursuing one without the other leads to spiritual ruin, pursuing one *in* the other leads to power and life. We see this interdependent relationship of Word and Spirit again and again throughout Scripture.

In the beginning, God established the world by His Word, but the Spirit hovered over the expanse and brought order and beauty to the firmament God had spoken into being. That's a good example of how the two relate: the Word issues the command and establishes the foundations; the Spirit quickens and makes alive.

The Spirit takes God's timeless truths and makes them come alive in us. He helps us understand them, shows us how to implement them, and empowers us to accomplish them. He transforms task lists into a relationship.

CLOSING PRAYER

Confess your tendency to settle for a Christian life centered on obeying tasks rather than cultivating a relationship. Ask God to take the truths you know and make them come alive in your heart.

THE GOSPEL OF GOD'S PRESENCE

God is everywhere. God is with us. God is always listening.

As Christians, we hear these truths and nod our heads. We believe these statements to be true, but we often don't feel the force of their truth. We know God promises to be with His people, and we know that in some way, He is present with us. But so many times, we don't sense His presence. We know He is close to us, so why does He seem so far away?

For some Christians, the solution is to seek different strategies to make His presence become more real to us. But that leads us to another question: What is His presence like? Some Christians are looking for that mysterious, tingly feeling whenever the music in a worship service crescendos at just the right time. Other Christians want a warm, Zen-like peace that floods their heart, assuring them that God is present and approves of their decisions. And then other Christians think God's presence is always manifested in grand and obvious ways—with miraculous healings, fainting spells, or physical trembling.

Perhaps we have two problems, not just one. The first problem is that God seems absent or distant. The second problem is that we don't know exactly what the presence of God is like, which is why we don't know when we are experiencing it. Put those two problems together, and it's no wonder many of us see the Christian life as a dutiful routine of "going through the motions" without experiencing the joy of our relationship with Christ.

In this week's study, we want to take a deeper look at the presence of God as a fundamental promise and benefit of the gospel. And as we proceed, we'll look at what it means to encounter the Holy Spirit and not only know He is in us, but sense His presence as He makes our hearts come alive to the gospel.

WARM UP

DISCUSSION STARTER: Christians believe that in the Person of the Holy Spirit, God is present with His people. As a group, answer the following:

Describe a time when you sensed the reality of God's presence.

What was it about that time that convinced you it was the Spirit working?

Do you think it is important for a Christian to not only believe God is with us, but also to sense His presence? Why or why not?

VIDEO TALKING POINTS

VIEW SESSION 2 on the DVD and use the following bullet points as a guide.

- God has always wanted to be present with His people.

- The Holy Spirit is God in us.

- Victorious Christianity can only be lived in the presence of God.

GROUP BIBLE STUDY
READ THE FOCAL PASSAGE: EPHESIANS 3:14-19

DISCUSS THE CONTEXT

The apostle Paul was writing to the church in Ephesus, explaining how God's plan has been to bring glory to Himself by (1) saving people by grace through faith, and (2) by incorporating all kinds of people, Jew and Gentile alike, into one body.

On Day 1 of last week's readings, we were asked to sum up this prayer from Paul in our own words. Discuss your summaries.

What are the main words or concepts from Paul's prayer that stood out to you in your summaries?

DISCUSS THE FOCAL VERSES

16 According to the riches of his glory he may grant you to be strengthened with power through his Spirit in your inner being, 17 so that Christ may dwell in your hearts through faith—that you, being rooted and grounded in love, 18 may have strength to comprehend with all the saints what is the breadth and length and height and depth, 19 and to know the love of Christ that surpasses knowledge, that you may be filled with all the fullness of God.
EPHESIANS 3:16-19

If Paul is praying for Christians who, by definition, already have the Holy Spirit dwelling in them, why do you think He prays in verses 16-17 for Christ and the Spirit to dwell in their hearts?

John Stott writes: "What Paul asks for his readers is that they may be 'fortified, braced, invigorated,' that they may 'know the strength of the Spirit's inner reinforcement,' and may lay hold ever more firmly 'by faith' of this divine strength, this divine indwelling."[1]

Why do you think it is important for us to experience by faith the reality of God dwelling in us?

APPLY GOD'S WORD

In what ways do fellow believers help us know and experience God's love? Why should believers seek greater knowledge of God's love together ("with all the saints") and not just on our own?

Notice the link between the gospel of Christ's love (vv. 18-19) and experiencing "the fullness of God" (v. 19). How does focusing on God's unmerited favor lead to being filled with His fullness?

Paul says the basis for strengthening our faith is that we are "rooted and grounded in love" (v. 17). What are some substitutes for the gospel we may be tempted to turn to in order to "jump start" the strengthening of our faith?

How can we encourage each other to renew our faith daily?

CLOSING PRAYER

Consider closing your group session by summarizing the discussion and then by praying this prayer from Clement of Rome (died A.D. 99) out loud as a group:

O God Almighty, Father of our Lord Jesus Christ,
grant us, we pray You, to be grounded and settled in Your truth
by the coming down of the Holy Spirit into our hearts.
That which we know not, do reveal.
That which is lacking in us, do fill up.
That which we know, do confirm.
And keep us blameless in Your service,
through the same Jesus Christ our Lord.[2]

Day 1

A GOD WHO WANTS US
JEREMIAH 23:23

If *Billboard* ranked church songs, "Jesus Loves Me" would probably be #1 on the preschool chart. From the time kids can put two sentences together, they're singing about Jesus' love for them—love we learn about in the Bible, love that overcomes our weaknesses, and love that welcomes the "little ones" who belong to His family. When the renowned theologian Karl Barth was asked to summarize his whole theology in one sentence, he replied: *Jesus loves me, this I know, for the Bible tells me so.* Profound truth expressed in simple words.

Unfortunately, we can sometimes get so familiar with just the statement of God's love that we miss the bigger picture of how this love is expressed.

> Romans 5:8 says, "God shows his love for us in that while we were still sinners, Christ died for us." Write down three or four reasons why God sent His Son to die for us.

God has demonstrated His love in sending His Son to die for us. But it's important to ask an additional question: *Why* did He send His Son to die? The Scriptures are clear that God wanted to bring us back to Himself, to reconcile us. Or to put it more simply: God wanted to be with us. He washed away our sin so He could welcome us into His presence.

God expresses love through His sacrificial actions in order to be with His people. Too many Christians get the first part of that truth ("God loves us") and even the second part ("through His sacrificial actions"), but then miss the purpose ("in order to be with His people"). The result is that we believe God loves us, but we don't think He likes us all that much.

Just like you probably have relatives who you "love" but don't necessarily like being around, you might think that God loves you like a distant father, someone who tolerates your imperfections and chastises you for your mistakes. He shows you grace in letting you live in his house, but he doesn't care to spend much time with you. Many of us have adopted this distorted picture of a God who loves us in the abstract, but who isn't very fond of us personally.

On a scale of 1-10, do you experience God's love for you as close and personal, or do you see Him as distant and abstract?

1   2   3   4   5   6   (7)   8   9   10
Distant and Abstract   *Close and Personal*

Contrast the distorted image of distant father with the God of the Bible, who from the beginning demonstrates a powerful desire to be with His people:

- In the garden of Eden, God walked with His people in the cool of the day (Gen. 3:8).
- After He saved the children of Israel from captivity in Egypt, God manifested His presence by leading them with a cloud by day and a pillar of fire by night (Ex. 13:21).
- God commanded Moses to construct a tabernacle, a place where He could pour out His presence in the midst of His people (Ex. 25:8-9).
- The Israelites often referred to God by His Name—Yahweh Shammah, which means "The LORD Is There" (Ezek. 48:35).
- Through the prophet Jeremiah, God said, "Am I a God at hand, declares the LORD, and not a God far away?" (Jer. 23:23).
- When the Messiah was promised, the angel said His name should be called "'Immanuel' (which means, God *with* us)" (Matt. 1:23).
- Jesus promised to send the Holy Spirit to dwell *in* us, so that God would be as real and present with us as Jesus was with His disciples (John 14:16-18).

Ours is not a God who loves in the abstract. This is a God who loves up close and personal. A God who wants to be near us.

What are some reasons you find it hard to believe that God not only loves you, but that He also likes you and wants to be with you?

CLOSING PRAYER

Ask God to help you see how He delights in you as a Father who loves and wants to be with His children.

Day 2

BELOVED SONS AND DAUGHTERS OF GOD
LUKE 3:21-22

Perhaps the most overlooked truth about the Holy Spirit is that His presence is intricately tied to the gospel. What is the gospel? It is the royal announcement that Jesus Christ, the Son of God, lived a perfect life in our place, died on the cross as a substitute for our sins, rose again to launch God's new creation, and is now exalted as King of the world. When we turn away from our sin and put our faith in Jesus and His work on our behalf, God forgives us and fully accepts us into His family.

The Holy Spirit is the One who makes this message intelligible to our hearts. When you became a Christian, the Spirit was there—convicting you of your sin, illuminating Christ and His work, and persuading you to believe. Once you believed, the Spirit then impressed upon your heart your new status as a beloved son or daughter of God, an adopted child warmly welcomed into God's family because of Christ.

The Spirit's work in your life didn't stop when you became a believer. He is still shining the light of Christ into your heart, helping you grow in your understanding of God's love for you. Fullness of the Spirit and depth of the gospel are inseparable, and one always leads you to the other. The more you grow in your understanding of the gospel, the more intimate you will become with the Spirit.

The Holy Spirit's descent upon Jesus at His baptism gives us a pattern for how we are to seek the fullness of the Spirit:

> [21] Now when all the people were baptized, and when Jesus also had been baptized and was praying, the heavens were opened, [22] and the Holy Spirit descended on him in bodily form, like a dove; and a voice came from heaven, "You are my beloved Son; with you I am well pleased."
> ### LUKE 3:21-22

How would you describe the relationship between the Holy Spirit's presence upon Jesus and the words of affirmation from heaven? Would it be possible to have one without the other?

Do you see how the fullness of the Spirit came simultaneously with the declaration of God's full pleasure in Jesus? In the gospel, the declaration God gave to Jesus that day by the Jordan River becomes ours. Because Jesus took our punishment, we share in His position before the Father (2 Cor. 5:21; Gal. 3:26-27). In Christ, God looks at us and says, "*You* are my beloved son [or daughter]; with you [because of Christ] I am well pleased." As we believe this, the Spirit falls on us, just as He did on Jesus. As He floods our heart, we feel the truth of that gospel intimately.

Perhaps you never heard your earthly father say, "I'm proud of you." Or maybe when you look into your heart and see your ongoing battle with certain sins, all you hear is the voice of the accuser, shouting at you about your failures and flaws. God's voice is louder. Let His voice drown out the others. What He says matters. The beauty of the gospel is that in Christ, we delight in God, and in Christ, God delights in us. He has loved us like He loves His Son!

> Is it easy or difficult for you to consider yourself a "beloved child" of God in whom He takes delight? Why?

Many times, we think that God will affirm us if we just do enough for Him. But notice how the Father's affirmation of Jesus took place *before* His public ministry began. Just as the affirmation of the Father preceded the work of the Son, so also God delights in you *before* you do anything for Him. Your life doesn't prove your love for God. Jesus' life proves God's love for you. We work because of God's love for us, not in order to win His love.

CLOSING PRAYER

Spend a few moments thanking God for the work of His Spirit in bringing you to faith and making you a beloved son or daughter.

Day 3

A GLIMPSE OF GOD'S GLORY
EXODUS 34:5-7

Look through the lyrics of many popular worship songs today, and you'll find requests to see God's glory, to have the eyes of our hearts opened, to experience God's presence. Strictly speaking, from the perspective of God's holiness and human sinfulness, these lyrics are asking for death. If an Israelite were to have barged into the temple and rushed into the holy of holies, he never would have come out. The presence of a holy God means death to a sinful man.

But there is something good and powerful about the desire to see God's glory. Moses himself, who already knew God's name and what God was like, wanted to know more. Not more facts about God or more details of His law. No, Moses wanted to *see* God's glory. And he was wise enough to know that he could only have such an experience if God made it possible.

So, on Mount Sinai, God put Moses in the cleft of a rock, covered him with His hand, and passed by in front of him. It's hard to imagine being more in the presence of God on earth than that! But note how Moses describes the situation:

> ⁵ Then the LORD came down in the cloud and stood there with him and proclaimed his name, the LORD. ⁶ And he passed in front of Moses, proclaiming, "The LORD, the LORD, the compassionate and gracious God, slow to anger, abounding in love and faithfulness,
> ⁷ maintaining love to thousands, and forgiving wickedness, rebellion and sin. Yet he does not leave the guilty unpunished ..."
> **EXODUS 34:5-7, NIV**

Write down a list of characteristics God uses to describe Himself in this passage.

Write down three things God has done in your life that are expressions of these characteristics.

This story gives us a picture of how God's presence comes into our lives today. God's Spirit declares God's name in our hearts, hiding us within the cross of Christ, rehearsing His mercy toward us, and making His holiness, justice, love, and glory come alive in our hearts.

It's not new knowledge about God that we gain, *per se*. It's often old knowledge becoming more real. Moses already *knew* God's name. But in that moment, he felt it. His face glowed for days as a result.

Describe a time when God took a biblical truth that you knew and made it become "more real" or "more alive" in your heart.

Would you say your Christian life is characterized more as a quest for gaining further knowledge about God or as a quest for deepening your experience of the knowledge you already have?

Why is it important that we not choose one of these options at the expense of the other?

The Puritan Thomas Goodwin explained how the Spirit makes biblical truth come alive in our hearts by describing the father-son relationship. Imagine a father walking along the road with a young son. Suddenly, the father picks him up, spins him around, kisses him, and says, "You know that I love you, I will never leave you, and I'm so proud you are my son!" Goodwin asks, "Was the boy any more his son in that moment than he was the moment before?"[3] Legally, no. But in that moment, the son *felt* his sonship in a new way. So it is with God's presence, Goodwin says. The fullness of the Spirit makes us *feel* the love of the gospel. Salvation goes from being a doctrine we believe to an embrace we receive from our Father. And just as Moses' face glowed from the experience, so our souls radiate with the joy and love of Christ.

CLOSING PRAYER

Ask the Spirit to transform you as you behold "the glory of the Lord" in the face of Christ (2 Cor. 4:4).

Day 4

THE GOSPEL OF THE PROMISED SPIRIT
JEREMIAH 31:33-34

Evangelicals like the word "saved." It's the way we describe what happens when we are converted, when we repent of our sin and trust in Jesus. We go from being "lost" to being "saved."

> If someone asked you what you mean by "being saved," what would you say? How would you explain the concept?

When we talk about "getting saved," we are usually referring to how we're saved *by* God *from* our sin, *by* God *from* eternal death. But where we stop, the Bible goes further. We're not just saved *by* God *from* sin. We're saved *for* something, as well. We are saved *for* a relationship with God (to know Him and love Him) and *for* His mission (His redeeming work to seek and save the lost). And it's the Holy Spirit who enables that relationship and empowers us for mission.

Take a look at this Old Testament text from the prophet Jeremiah about what conversion will be like after the Messiah comes:

> ³³ For this is the covenant that I will make with the house of Israel after those days, declares the LORD: I will put my law within them, and I will write it on their hearts. And I will be their God, and they shall be my people. ³⁴ And no longer shall each one teach his neighbor and each his brother, saying, 'Know the LORD,' for they shall all know me, from the least of them to the greatest, declares the LORD. For I will forgive their iniquity, and I will remember their sin no more.
> **JEREMIAH 31:33-34**

In this passage, God is making a promise to save His people. As you walk through each aspect of God's promise, write down two or three of our needs or problems that require God to intervene in this way.

Let's start with what we're saved *from*. Look again at verse 34: "For I will forgive their wrongdoing and never again remember their sin" (HCSB). Glory to God for His purposeful forgetfulness! Isn't that the beauty of the gospel? God promises to forgive us and never bring up our sins again.

But note the promise that comes just before that verse: "They will all know Me, from the least to the greatest of them" (HCSB). And just before that: "I will put my law within them, and I will write it on their hearts. And I will be their God, and they shall be my people."

See the context? It's not just forgiveness of sins. It's new hearts resulting in a restored relationship. As we saw in last week's readings, Ezekiel prophesied along the same lines—God will cleanse you of sin, deliver you from idolatry, *and place His Spirit within you* (Ezek. 36:25-26). In other words, not only will God wipe away our sins, He also will give us His Spirit, restore our relationship with Him, and enable us to obey. The promise of the gospel is not just that we are forgiven, but that we are made new.

> What is the danger of focusing only on what we're saved "from" to the neglect of what we're saved "for"?

With the Old Testament promises in the background, it's no wonder that in his sermon at Pentecost, Peter moved from proclamation of Jesus to proclamation of the promise of the Spirit:

> [38] Repent and be baptized, every one of you, in the
> name of Jesus Christ for the forgiveness of your sins.
> And you will receive the gift of the Holy Spirit.
> **ACTS 2:38, NIV**

Forgiveness of sins is only half of the promise. When we repent and believe, God doesn't just clean up a bad heart; through the Spirit, He gives us a new heart. It's not that God does open-heart surgery. He gives us a heart transplant. God doesn't just wipe the slate clean of our disobedience; He indwells us so that we will long for obedience. He doesn't just offer His forgiveness; He offers Himself—in relationship to us.

CLOSING PRAYER

Spend some time praising God for (1) being the One who saved you, (2) from sin, death, and hell, and (3) for a renewed relationship with Himself through His Spirit.

Day 5
THE FRUITFULNESS OF FRIENDSHIP
GALATIANS 5:22-23

Imagine a friendship where the focus is always on your responsibilities to one another. You have the responsibility to call and check up on each other every day. You must meet face to face at least three times a week. You are required to send an encouraging note whenever your friend is discouraged. Every holiday or birthday requires a gift. Imagine two friends who dutifully check off their list of responsibilities, making sure they fulfill all the requirements of their friendship.

Now imagine a friendship where the focus is on your relationship with one another. As you cultivate your friendship and get to know your friend, you find yourself calling to make sure things are going well. You try to get together as often as possible. When you notice your friend is down, you figure out ways to encourage. You're always thinking of the next gift for the next holiday.

What's the difference between the two friendships? The first is focused on the responsibilities. The second is focused on the relationship. In the first scenario, you fulfill the responsibilities of the friendship but don't necessarily have much of a relationship. In the second scenario, you get both. You focus on the relationship, and the responsibilities follow naturally.

On a scale of 1-10, is your relationship with God closer to scenario 1 or closer to scenario 2?

| 1 | 2 | 3 | 4 | 5 | 6 | 7 | 8 | 9 | 10 |

Responsibility-Focused   *Relationship-Focused*

Take a moment to read from Galatians, where Paul describes the fruit of the Spirit:

> [22] But the fruit of the Spirit is love, joy, peace, forbearance, kindness, goodness, faithfulness, [23] gentleness and self-control. Against such things there is no law.
> **GALATIANS 5:22-23, NIV**

Why do you think Paul uses the singular word "fruit" instead of the plural "fruits" before giving this list?

Do you think it is possible to fully excel at any of these descriptors without the others? Why or why not?

Think about Paul's analogy of fruit. Fruits on a plant are the natural result of its being alive. When the Spirit is alive in us, His fruit will grow *naturally* in our hearts. The more we know God, Paul says, the larger the Spirit's presence in our heart, and the larger His presence, the more His fruit begins to abound in our lives. We don't produce fruit by working it up with self-discipline and resolve. We simply drive our roots deeply into the gospel and the fruit naturally grows.

Think of how a married couple produces physical "fruit." In the moment of conception, they are not thinking about the mechanics of making the child; they are swept up in love for one another! The "fruit" of that is a child. In a similar manner, when we get swept up in intimate interaction with Jesus in the gospel, the "fruit" that results is love, joy, peace, patience, kindness, goodness, gentleness and self-control. Spiritual fruit comes not by concentrating on producing those attributes, but by becoming intimately aware of God's full acceptance of us in the gospel.

What are some ways you can move your focus from your responsibilities as a Christian to your relationship with Christ?

Jonathan Edwards compared the Spirit's illumination of the gospel to the experience of tasting honey for someone who had never tasted sweetness. No words can capture the sensation of sweetness bursting alive on the tongue for the first time.[4] Such moments are more than "flashes of insight." They are, as the apostle John explains, communion with God Himself (1 John 1). In those moments the Spirit is making the gospel personal to you.

The gospel is an invitation to *relationship*. To study biblical doctrine is never an end in itself; it's what points us to God's heart. The more we know what God has done for us, the more our hearts should come alive to Him personally. To fail to interact with the Spirit of God in our study of biblical doctrine is to miss the real purpose.

CLOSING PRAYER

Ask God to help you sense the waves of His love washing over you as you reflect on His grace in the gospel. Ask Him to bear fruit in and through you today as you focus on Him.

SURRENDERED TO THE SPIRIT FOR MISSION

If you're like us, you've spent a significant part of your Christian life feeling guilty over what you are not doing in the kingdom of God.

You've heard the calls to radical living and sacrificial generosity, and you've stepped up your efforts to make a difference. But even when you're involved in the church, supporting missionary efforts, and giving time and money to the disadvantaged, you still feel like it's just a drop in the bucket. The two of us have spent significant time doing mission work in other parts of the world, and still we feel like whatever we do seems so small and insignificant compared to the monumental task we've been given.

That's when the doubts creep in. *Maybe I'm not doing enough for the Lord. Even the best I can offer of my time, talents, or possessions is minuscule compared to the need! Am I wasting resources on myself instead of God's kingdom? Is it my fault I'm not making a big enough difference?* These questions slowly sap you of your spiritual energy. The more you dwell on the needs, the less motivated you are to get involved. Who wants to try to empty the ocean with a thimble?

In this session, we're going to tackle this problem by realizing that the solution resides in a counter-intuitive truth: *God doesn't need you.* We vastly overestimate what we have to contribute. We don't have "more" we need to give; we actually have nothing God needs to begin with. Nothing.

Here's the good news: Even though God doesn't need us, He wants to work through us and through the gifts He's given us. And that's why we need to extend our gaze beyond the needs of the world to the Spirit's empowering presence in our lives.

WARM UP

DISCUSSION STARTER: The call to take the gospel to the nations and to share the generous love of Christ can be overwhelming when we are faced with the needs of our world.

What do you think is the bigger problem for the church today when it comes to fulfilling our mission: Apathy and indifference? Or weariness and burnout?

In what ways might these two problems (apathy vs. weariness) be related?

VIDEO TALKING POINTS

VIEW SESSION 3 on the DVD and use the following bullet points as a guide.

- God doesn't need you—never has, never will.

- God doesn't look to us and say, "I need you to save the world *for* Me." He calls us to follow Him as He saves the world *through* us.

- We need to get away from "good" ideas in ministry and start to pursue "God" ideas—Acts 8.

- Are you following the Spirit in mission?

- Have you determined what the Spirit of God wants from you?

GROUP BIBLE STUDY
READ THE FOCAL PASSAGE: JOHN 14:12-14

DISCUSS THE CONTEXT

Jesus spoke these words as part of His instruction to His disciples in the hours before He would suffer and die for the sins of the world.

> Based on the context of these verses, what do you think it means for Jesus to do "whatever" the disciples asked in His name?

> According to verse 13, what should be the goal of everything we ask in Jesus' name?

DISCUSS THE FOCAL VERSE

> 12 Truly, truly, I say to you, whoever believes in me will also do the works that I do; and greater works than these will he do, because I am going to the Father.
> **JOHN 14:12**

> Jesus said that whoever believes in Him will do the works He does. What "works" do you think Jesus is referring to?

> How do Jesus' words about His disciples doing "greater works" than He did strike you? How is it possible for our works to be "greater" than the works Jesus did?

There are two ways in which our works are "greater" than those of Jesus. Jesus' miraculous works were a signpost toward the deeper reality of conversion. For example, when Jesus raised a paralyzed man, He did so in order to prove that He had the power to forgive sins (Mark 2:1-11). Forgiving sins was the point; healing was just a sign. Whenever we persuade people to believe in Jesus, the Spirit is accomplishing through us a work that is greater than healing.

The second way our works are "greater" refers to the range of our works. When Jesus was on earth, the Holy Spirit focused His ministry on one individual. Today, He is in every believer. And the collective impact of ordinary Christians filled with the Spirit is greater than if Jesus Himself had stayed on earth.

APPLY GOD'S WORD

If the secret of the Christian life is Christ *in* me, not Christ *and* me, how can we cultivate an attitude of willingness to discover what the Spirit wants to do through us individually?

How can we help each other discover what Christ wants to do through us?

How we can we stop seeing just the needs of the world and start seeing the power we have through the Spirit's presence?

What can we do to encourage and strengthen each other when we feel overwhelmed by the enormity of God's mission?

CLOSING PRAYER

Consider closing your group session by summarizing the discussion and then by praying this prayer from Apollonius (A.D. 170-245) out loud as a group:

O Lord Jesus Christ, give us Your Spirit
that we may be enabled to obey Your teaching:
to pacify anger, to take part in pity,
to moderate desire, to increase love,
to put away sorrow, to cast away vain glory,
not to be vindictive, not to fear death;
ever entrusting our spirit to the immortal God
who with You and the Holy Spirit lives and reigns world without end.[1]

Day 1
THE EASY BURDEN
MATTHEW 11:28-30

We've found that many, if not most, committed Christians spend a lot of their Christian life feeling overwhelmed by guilt over what they are not doing in the kingdom of God. They've been told to be radical, full of "crazy love," followers of Jesus rather than fans—and these are all true and needed messages. And yet many of us, after a really zealous start, end up feeling paralyzed by the weight of it all. So we toggle between summers of feverish activity and winters of guilt and fatigue.

But then we come across passages of Scripture where Jesus says things like this:

> 28 Come to me, all who labor and are heavy laden, and I will give you rest. 29 Take my yoke upon you, and learn from me, for I am gentle and lowly in heart, and you will find rest for your souls. 30 For my yoke is easy, and my burden is light.
> ## MATTHEW 11:28-30

If you were to pick three words or phrases to describe your Christian life, what would they be?

Which of your words line up with what Scripture teaches the Christian life should be like? Which of your words do not?

The reason Jesus can give us a monumental mission (take the gospel to all nations) and still describe His burden as easy and light is because of one thing—or better said, one Person. The Holy Spirit is the One who works *through* us. Too often, we see ourselves as Jesus' helper, when Jesus said the Spirit would be *our* Helper.

God is not now, nor has He ever, looked for "helpers" to assist Him in saving the world. That doesn't mean He isn't calling us to give ourselves generously to that mission or be sacrificially generous with our neighbors; it's just that He's not looking for people to supply His needs. He's not short on money, talent, or time. He has never commanded us to go save the world *for* Him; He calls us to *follow* Him as He saves the world *through* us.

In what areas of your life do you feel "heavy laden" and in need of rest?

God doesn't call to us from a place of need; we call to Him. Why do we often see our involvement in His mission as if it is the other way around?

Instead of asking the question, *What needs to be done in the world?* we must ask, *What is the Spirit of God leading me to do?* Just like Jesus told His apostles to wait on the coming of the Holy Spirit before they went out to the world, we are to look to the Holy Spirit for His direction in what God would have us do.

The weight of responsibility for the mission does not rest on our shoulders, but on Jesus' shoulders. He leads; we follow. He commands; we obey. He supplies; we steward. He delivers; we worship. Try to switch roles and you'll live a life of guilt-laden burnout instead of sustained, joy-filled, life-giving sacrifice.

What is the relationship between learning from Jesus and finding "rest for your souls" (v. 29)?

How is the "rest" Jesus calls us to different than the complacency of the world?

How is the "work" Jesus calls us to different than bursts of spiritual busyness?

CLOSING PRAYER

Ask the Lord to renew and refresh you today with the knowledge that apart from Him, you can do nothing. Ask Him to reveal areas in your life where you see yourself as "helping God" rather than God working through you.

Day 2
CHRIST IN ME
COLOSSIANS 1:27

Guilt-driven Christianity leads to burnout, whether it's feeling guilty because you're not doing enough for God's kingdom or because you continue to struggle against so many entangling sins. Guilt is also a huge demotivator for service in God's kingdom. *I'm just not good enough yet, not Christ-like enough yet! If you only knew all the sins I battle on a daily basis! God wouldn't use me, because He could have His pick from so many Christians who are better than me!*

If it's not the great needs of the world that overwhelm you, it's the great sins of your heart that threaten to keep you from God's mission. Your idea of those living on mission is victorious Christians who have, if not fully at least satisfactorily, gained victory over the bigger sins in their lives and can now focus outwardly on the world around them. They've won the inner battle; now they can look outside.

> Which feeling of guilt demotivates you from participating in God's mission more: feeling guilty for not doing enough for God's kingdom or feeling guilty for the sins you still battle? How does that feeling affect your passion for God's kingdom?

When Jesus commissioned His disciples on the mountain after His resurrection, He told them they would take the gospel from "Jerusalem and in all Judea and Samaria, and to the ends of the earth" (Acts 1:8). This was a ragtag group of men who weren't the most educated or most financially endowed, and yet the need of the world didn't overcome them. If anyone could have looked at the task and said, "It's too big and we can't handle it!" it should have been them, right? We've got more opportunities to spread the gospel today than they did, and yet they didn't balk at the task. Why not?

Perhaps we can find the answer in the verses surrounding the Great Commission text (Matt. 28:19-20). Just before Jesus tells His disciples to go into the world and "make disciples," He makes this statement: "All authority in heaven and on earth has been given to Me" (v. 18). And after He commissions the disciples, He makes this promise: "And behold, I am with you always, to the end of the age" (v. 20).

What effect do you think Jesus' statement of authority and Jesus' promise of His presence made on the disciples, when considering the mammoth task they had been given?

What role does faith in Jesus' promise of presence play in helping us overcome our feelings of inadequacy?

Jesus didn't commission perfect people back then, and He doesn't commission perfect people now. Peter would later compromise his witness to the gospel and would be confronted by Paul. The early Christian churches battled false teaching (Galatians), dealt with immorality (Jude), struggled for unity (Corinthians), and forgot their hope (Thessalonians). And yet through these churches and their leaders, the gospel went forth. What was the secret? Christ was in them. In his letter to the Colossians, Paul wrote:

> 27 To them God chose to make known how great
> among the Gentiles are the riches of the glory of this
> mystery, which is Christ in you, the hope of glory.
> **COLOSSIANS 1:27**

Too many times, we see the Christian life as something we are doing *for* God. Nothing will wear you out more than thinking the mission is all on you. Others feel like it's Christ *and* me, like we're wrestling against the Devil and whenever we need Him to take over, Jesus comes into the ring and takes a few swings. The Scriptures remind us that it's Christ *in* us who brings victory.

Take a few minutes to read Romans 8, Paul's chapter on the victorious life of a believer. Count how many times he refers to the Spirit. What does this tell us about our need for the Spirit as we battle our sinful flesh?

CLOSING PRAYER

Confess your sins and feelings of guilt, and ask God to make you aware of Christ's power in you through the Holy Spirit.

Day 3
A POSTURE OF SURRENDER
I SAMUEL 15:22

"I just don't know what God wants from me." Many a Christian has spoken these words, confused about the way forward, perplexed about the will of God. Looking for Scripture might not lead us to the specific plan of God for our lives (you won't find who God wants you to marry or where God wants you to go to college by reading the Minor Prophets!), but Scripture does tell us what God's will is. It doesn't describe a specific plan but a type of posture.

When Paul summed up in Romans what God wants from us, he called for grateful sacrifice and complete surrender:

> [1] Therefore, I urge you, brothers and sisters, in view of God's mercy, to offer your bodies as a living sacrifice, holy and pleasing to God—this is your true and proper worship.
> **ROMANS 12:1, NIV**

We are to offer our bodies as living sacrifices to God as an *act of worship*. Notice that we do this in response to something—*the mercies of God*. The mercies of God in the gospel, Paul believes, should cause us to be so overwhelmed with gratefulness that we joyfully die to everything we have wanted from life so that we can live to fulfill His desires.

God wants us to have a posture of surrender and sacrifice. Following Jesus means a full surrender of our wills to God. In the Old Testament, the first king of Israel—Saul—failed terribly at this. Rather than giving God what He asked for, Saul offered a substitute—although a generous one—in place of surrender. God rebuked Saul with these harsh words:

> But Samuel replied: "Does the LORD delight in burnt offerings and sacrifices as much as in obeying the LORD? To obey is better than sacrifice, and to heed is better than the fat of rams.
> **I SAMUEL 15:22, NIV**

God calls us to surrender everything to Him, but we are often tempted to offer substitutes. What kind of substitutes are we likely to rely on in place of full surrender?

The first command Jesus gave for those who follow Him is the complete surrender of our wills. He said:

> Whoever wants to be my disciple must deny themselves
> and take up their cross and follow me.
> **MATTHEW 16:24, NIV**

In your own words, how would you define "deny yourself"?

Why is it impossible to follow Jesus and not deny yourself?

"Deny yourself" means a total surrender of every desire in your heart to God. Every dream, every desire, every ambition. You say "no" to all that you want from life so that you are ready to say "yes" to all that He wants from it.

"Take up your cross" means you embrace God's agenda in life rather than your own. The cross is the best-known Christian symbol, but for many Christians it has become little more than a sentimental piece of jewelry to hang around their necks. For the first disciples, it was no piece of jewelry. The cross was an instrument of oppression, torture, pain, and death with which they were very familiar. Crosses struck fear into the hearts of all who beheld them.

To follow Jesus means that you die to any control you maintain over your life. Like a man on a cross, you place yourself under Jesus' complete domination, with no dreams of your own for your future. Dead men have no more ambition for their lives. We die to ourselves and the Spirit makes us alive to Christ. It's a daily putting to death of our own ambitions and a daily realignment with His will for us.

CLOSING PRAYER

Ask God to help you present your life to Him in this way—with no conditions or restrictions.

51

Day 4
A POSTURE OF SACRIFICE
2 SAMUEL 24:24

We've seen that God's will is for us to have a posture of surrender and a posture of sacrifice. In contrast to King Saul's lack of surrender, David yielded himself to God. Whatever God would command, David stood ready to obey. When the prophet Nathan told David what God wanted from him, he obeyed with great zeal. His exuberance in obedience became so contagious that he brought all of Israel along with him into his offering (1 Chron. 22:2-19).

> When have you witnessed or been part of a group of people
> whose passion for a cause aligned for a common purpose?

David's posture of surrender led also to a posture of sacrifice. He felt so overwhelmed at what God had done for him that his heart overflowed with a desire to give back to God. That's why David wanted to build the Lord a temple. This request pleased God, and even though God reserved the temple building for David's son, Solomon, God did allow David to collect the materials for building. The writer of Chronicles records that he provided a large amount of materials, "without number," and "with great pains" to himself (1 Chron. 22:4,14).

A heart that truly understands the gospel overflows with gratefulness for God. Extravagant grace produces extravagant givers.

> When was the last time you gave of time and money in a
> way that went above and beyond your normal giving? What
> prompted you to give more than usual?

David knew he had been nothing when God chose him to be king: a shepherd, the lowliest occupation in Israel, and the "least" of eight sons. God had given him *everything*. And even more than an earthly kingship, God had given him forgiveness of sins and an eternal inheritance. David's heart burst with grateful thanksgiving.

> ¹⁸ Who am I, Sovereign LORD, and what is my
> family, that you have brought me this far?
>
> **2 SAMUEL 7:18, NIV**

In the space below, write down two or three milestones in your life that are expressions of how God has brought you this far. Then, spend a few minutes thanking God for His kindness toward you.

Consider the kindness of God toward you. Where would you be had Jesus not come to earth to save you? He had no obligation to come. What were you when He came for you? You were condemned, having sold yourself to sin. Yet, He voluntarily absorbed the sting of your rejection and died in shame upon a cross in your place, going through hell itself for you, so you could live with Him in indescribable joy forever.

When you understand God's goodness to you, it changes your attitude toward life. How could it not? Extravagant generosity compels extravagant response. When we realize how much God has given us, we become willing servants, eager to be poured out for God and His kingdom.

Toward the end of his life, David wanted again to give something to God—a field on which God would construct the temple. The owner told David he could just have it. But David responded:

> ²⁴ No, I insist on paying you for it. I will not sacrifice to the
> LORD my God burnt offerings that cost me nothing.
>
> **2 SAMUEL 24:24, NIV**

David would not give to God an offering that cost him nothing because by this point he understood well that his offerings were not about meeting God's needs, but about expressing God's worthiness. If the gift had been about meeting God's needs, then a free field would suffice. But to give God a gift that cost David nothing would not express to God how he felt about Him.

What would a posture of grateful sacrifice look like in your life?

CLOSING PRAYER

Ask God to help you express your gratitude and His worthiness through your life as a sacrifice.

Day 5

YOUR AGENDA VS. GOD'S AGENDA
MARK 1:15

What is repentance? Most people think it has something to do with shedding tears of sorrow for past actions or attitudes. It's feeling sorry for your sins, combined with a desire to change. There's no doubt that feeling genuine sorrow for your sins is part of repentance, but what if we're missing another vitally important aspect?

When Jesus began His ministry, He preached a message of repentance in light of the coming kingdom of God:

> [15] The time is fulfilled, and the kingdom of God is
> at hand; repent and believe in the gospel.
> **MARK 1:15**

> In your own words, how would you explain to someone what it means to "repent and believe in the gospel"? Write your answer below.

To "repent" means to turn around, to change direction. It includes an element of reversal. It's impossible to repent and stay the same. It would defy the definition of the word.

So what direction do we take? Notice that the call to repentance comes right after Jesus proclaims something: the arrival of God's kingdom. God's rule and reign is breaking into human history, and this kingdom is coming through Jesus—the King. Within this context, repentance doesn't simply mean weeping over our sins; it means we turn around, abandon our own kingdom agendas, and adopt the kingdom agenda of Jesus Christ. To repent is to sign up for God's kingdom—to be part of His people who are about His business in the world.

> Take a moment to describe an ordinary unbeliever's hopes and dreams for life. What does it look like for someone apart from God to build their own personal "kingdom" in this life?

Write down three or four of the most powerful hopes and dreams you have for your life. How similar or different are they from the unbeliever's?

There are three ways we respond to God's kingdom agenda. The first is to pit our agenda against God's. This is the posture of the people in Genesis 11, who sought to build a city and a tower up to the sky in order to make a name for themselves. Their desire was to set up a rival kingdom, apart from God and His power. The default position for every human being on earth is to set up a personal kingdom where we are in control of our lives, our choices, and our destiny—*our agenda versus God's*.

The second way we respond to God's kingdom agenda is by adding it to ours. This is the option many Christians take. We have our own agenda, which is altered by God's in that we have incorporated some of God's heartfelt desires into our own. We *add* God's kingdom agenda to our own. Or we ask God to bless our own agenda as we adopt bits and pieces of His—*our agenda alongside God's*.

The third way we respond to God's kingdom agenda is by allowing His to replace ours. His missionary heart is reflected in our missionary heart. His hopes and dreams for the world become ours. This isn't about adding God's agenda to our own; it's about the fusion of God's heart and ours.

This is what it means to be surrendered to the Spirit. The Spirit is not who we invoke to give power to our own plans. He is the One who introduces us to God's plans. We look to see where God is working and what God wants to do, and we join Him in fulfilling *His* mission. *God's agenda becomes our agenda.*

Which of the three responses to God's kingdom agenda best sums up your posture of repentance?

What are some ways you can better align yourself with God's heart for this world, and thus, have His agenda replace our own?

CLOSING PRAYER

Ask God to forgive you for altering or adding His kingdom agenda to your own, and pray that He will help you adopt a posture of surrender to His Spirit and His mission.

YOU
ARE GIFTED

We know what God's will is for us *generally*.
He wants us to know Him and make Him known.

He wants us to pursue holiness through a posture of surrender and sacrifice. He wants us to live on mission, according to His kingdom agenda, not ours.

But how do we discern what God's will is for us *specifically?* What does God want *from you?* We know what God wants from believers in general, but what does God expect of us in this time and place? How can we be sure we're doing the right things for God? How can we know we are fulfilling His will?

The good news is the Scriptures give us guidance in how to discern the specifics of what God wants from us, and this discernment includes following the guidance of the Holy Spirit. The Holy Spirit appears 59 times in Acts, and in 36 of those, He is speaking, guiding and instructing. John Newton, the Puritan who wrote the lyrics to "Amazing Grace" once asked, in effect, "Is it really true that the leadership of the Spirit, upon which the early church so depended on for success—has become irrelevant to us today?"[1]

In this session, we will begin to discover the ways we are guided by the Spirit. Through the gospel, we experience the fullness of the Spirit, first by receiving Him in faith and then growing full of Him as we deepen our understanding of what God has done for us in Christ. Through God's Word, we receive guidance from the Spirit. He also works through our personal gifts, the church, our spirit, and our circumstances—but never in ways that contradict what God's Word clearly says.

WARM UP

DISCUSSION STARTER: Ask everyone in your group either about their current or former occupation.

How many different kinds of work are represented among the people in your group?

How does each occupation contribute to the benefit of society?

What would be missing if there were no one to fulfill these roles in our culture?

VIDEO TALKING POINTS

VIEW SESSION 4 on the DVD and use the following bullet points as a guide.

■ Do you know what your spiritual gift is?

■ Affinity: things you're really passionate about.

■ Ability: something you find yourself naturally good at.

■ Affirmation: what people in the church tell you that God is using you to do in their lives.

■ A spiritual gift is an unusual effectiveness in a responsibility given to all believers.

■ Being guilt-driven can crush you and paralyze you, but being gift-driven becomes empowering and liberating.

Video sessions available for purchase at
www.lifeway.com/JesusContinued

GROUP BIBLE STUDY
READ THE FOCAL PASSAGE: I CORINTHIANS 12:4-7

DISCUSS THE CONTEXT

The Corinthian congregation was deeply divided. Some of the believers were divided over whose leadership to follow. Other believers were divided because they saw their spiritual gifts as more important than the others.

> Why is it important for believers to embrace both the variety of spiritual gifts and the truth that these gifts all come from God?

> How is our work hindered when we lift up certain gifts to the exclusion or neglect of others?

DISCUSS THE FOCAL VERSE

> [7] To each is given the manifestation of the Spirit for the common good.
> **I CORINTHIANS 12:7**

Take a look at different ways "manifestation of the Spirit" can be translated:
"the manifestation of the Spirit" (ESV, NIV, KJV, NASB);
"a demonstration of the Spirit" (HCSB);
"The Spirit has given ... a special way of serving others" (CEV);
"The Spirit's presence is shown in some way" (GNT);
"a spiritual gift is given" (NLT).

> What are the different nuances that each of these translations bring out from the original language?

> According to this verse, what is the purpose of this "manifestation of the Spirit" in our gifts?

What happens when we seek to exercise spiritual gifts without consideration of the "common good" of the body of Christ?

What goes wrong when we seek spiritual gifts in order to display our own power or praise instead of manifesting the Spirit?

APPLY GOD'S WORD

Why is it important to not think of spiritual gifts as representative of a class of "super-Christians" but something God grants us all?

How is our mission affected by thinking the Holy Spirit's work is only through leaders and not every church member?

How can we lovingly affirm the spiritual gifts we see in others?

When was the last time you benefited from a believer's exercise of a spiritual gift? How did his or her actions strengthen you?

CLOSING PRAYER

Consider closing your group session by summarizing the discussion and then by praying this prayer from B. H. Carroll (1843-1914) out loud as a group:

O blessed Spirit of God, the administrator of Jesus Christ, breathe on your church and let the inspiration of the Almighty enter it! Let us feel that you are a presence, a presence that can be known, a presence that will comfort, a presence that will protect, a presence that will shine on heaven and make it glitter like diamonds, a presence that will shine on death and make it a portal of glory. So, Spirit of God, breathe on us![2]

Day 1

GUILT-DRIVEN VS. GIFT-DRIVEN
ROMANS 12:6

Whenever you feel guilty about the massive needs you see in the world, you are likely to take on assignments based on whatever bothers you most at the present time. Your guilt pushes and pulls you this way and that, and you choose tasks based on whatever makes you feel better, or whatever makes you feel like you're meeting the need.

The problem is that a guilt-driven approach to service is all about you. The guilt you feel drives you to action, and then the action lessens (at least temporarily) some of that guilt. You may be helping others in great ways, but you're motivated more by the burden *you feel* than by the relief others receive.

That's why "guilt-driven motivation" produces frustration and burnout. It's more self-focused than it appears on the surface.

> Think of two or three avenues of ministry or service you have been involved in. What was your motivation for participating? How can you tell?

God wants us to participate in His mission, not from a feeling of guilt, but from the reality of gifting. A "gift-driven" environment produces empowerment, confidence, and joy. Why? Just think: if you knew God had *appointed* you to do something, and had *anointed* you for it, and was *working* in you to accomplish it, wouldn't that produce an enormous amount of confidence?

> *Anointed* is a word Christians throw around to mean a person has a special endowment of the Holy Spirit's power. But Paul speaks of "anointing" as the birthright of every believer. How difficult or easy is it for you to think of yourself as "anointed" by God to do something for His kingdom? Why?

Too many of us settle for feeling guilty about what we're not gifted to do, or we become envious of gifts God has given to others but not us. Like feuding children on Christmas morning, we tear open our presents, take a look at what we've been given, and then immediately begin comparing our gifts to those that others received. We ignore something Paul made clear in his letter to the Romans:

> ⁶ Having gifts that differ according to the
> grace given to us, let us use them.
> **ROMANS 12:6a**

How does the nature of the gifts you've received help you make decisions about the best way to serve God's people?

Each of us has particular assignments that God has given us. Our role in His kingdom is to execute those gifts faithfully. In doing so, we are part of a body that is doing all the wonderful things Jesus is doing on earth. You may never personally take care of orphans in Uganda, but in using your gifts faithfully, you are part of a body that does. This is not, of course, to excuse a callous heart toward things that don't interest you. We should pray for and support those who are doing things we are not called to, and we should always be open to God's revealing to us new ways He can use us to bless others in His name. But the focus of our life needs to be built around using whatever gifts God has given us in the places that need them most.

When people would come to him wondering what God's will was for their lives, John Stott was known to say: "Go wherever your gifts will be most exploited for God's kingdom." In other words, discern your gifts, and find where they intersect with a need in the world. And then get busy.

Do you want to walk with the Spirit? Do you want to experience the exhilaration of being used in divine power? If so, then pursue your spiritual gifts, because spiritual gifts are the manifestation of the Spirit's power and presence in you.

CLOSING PRAYER
Ask God to help you move from a guilt-driven approach to a gift-driven way of seeing ministry opportunities.

Day 2

THE SPIRIT'S GIFTS
I CORINTHIANS 12:8-11; ROMANS 12:6-8; EPHESIANS 4:7,11-16

God's Spirit bestows upon each believer *pneumatika* (1 Cor. 12:1-4). We typically translate that word as "spiritual gift," but it literally says "a spiritual." It implies something like a "spiritual manifestation" or a "spiritual experience" and doesn't translate well into English. God gives to us, and to others through us, *experiences* with the Spirit through the *pneumatika* He distributes to each of us. Through these *pneumatika* the Spirit Himself touches people, cares for them, ministers to them, and speaks to them.

If you are a believer, you have *pneumatika*. In Romans 12:6, Paul calls them grace gifts (*charismata*) and says God has placed a few specific ones in your heart for His purposes. Through them, God *Himself* works through you. So you can know more about what God wants from you, specifically, by getting to know your gifts.

In three primary passages, Paul lists out various spiritual gifts:

> [8] For to one is given through the Spirit the utterance of wisdom, and to another the utterance of knowledge according to the same Spirit, [9] to another faith by the same Spirit, to another gifts of healing by the one Spirit, [10] to another the working of miracles, to another prophecy, to another the ability to distinguish between spirits, to another various kinds of tongues, to another the interpretation of tongues. [11] All these are empowered by one and the same Spirit, who apportions to each one individually as he wills.
> ### I CORINTHIANS 12:8-11

> [6] Having gifts that differ according to the grace given to us, let us use them: if prophecy, in proportion to our faith; [7] if service, in our serving; the one who teaches, in his teaching; [8] the one who exhorts, in his exhortation; the one who contributes, in generosity; the one who leads, with zeal; the one who does acts of mercy, with cheerfulness.
> ### ROMANS 12:6-8

⁷ But grace was given to each one of us according to the measure of Christ's gift. ... ¹¹ And he gave the apostles, the prophets, the evangelists, the shepherds and teachers, ¹² to equip the saints for the work of ministry, for building up the body of Christ, ¹³ until we all attain to the unity of the faith and of the knowledge of the Son of God, to mature manhood, to the measure of the stature of the fullness of Christ, ¹⁴ so that we may no longer be children, tossed to and fro by the waves and carried about by every wind of doctrine, by human cunning, by craftiness in deceitful schemes. ¹⁵ Rather, speaking the truth in love, we are to grow up in every way into him who is the head, into Christ, ¹⁶ from whom the whole body, joined and held together by every joint with which it is equipped, when each part is working properly, makes the body grow so that it builds itself up in love.

EPHESIANS 4:7,11-16

Make a list of the spiritual gifts mentioned in these passages. What similarities do you see? What differences?

None of the lists are identical, and each contains a few the others leave out. This shows us that spiritual gifts are not so much a defined set of functions as much as they are various manifestations of God using us in the lives of others. We are not to list out these gifts on a spreadsheet and assume they comprise the full scope of all that God empowers His people to do. Each list simply gives examples of how God works through His people. There are likely others not mentioned in any of Paul's lists.

Reread Ephesians 4:14-16 and summarize in your own words the reason why God gives different gifts to His people.

Pick three gifts from your list and write down what would happen if they were used in ways that did not align with the purpose God lays out in Ephesians 4:14-16.

CLOSING PRAYER

Ask God to help you identify your spiritual gifts and affirm the gifts you see in others so that your church can be strengthened by His grace.

Day 3
IDENTIFYING YOUR SPIRITUAL GIFTS
I CORINTHIANS 12:1-4

One of the ways we discern God's will for our lives is by discerning the gifts He has given us. In this way, we answer the question "What does God want me to do?" with another question, "What gifts has God given you?" Here are several principles to help you discover the answer to that second question, which will then illuminate the answer to the first.

I. A SPIRITUAL GIFT GENERATES AN UNUSUAL EFFECTIVENESS IN A RESPONSIBILITY GIVEN TO ALL BELIEVERS.

"I don't have the gift of evangelism," some Christians say. "Therefore, I don't have to evangelize." Wrong. Most of the spiritual gifts (like evangelism) are assigned to all believers. For example, God commands all believers to serve, evangelize, prophesy, pray for healing, intercede for others, trust God for provision, be generous, exhort one another, and so on. We don't get a pass on these things just because we don't feel particularly gifted in one area or another.

At the same time, we all recognize that some believers are particularly effective in these gifts. This person may excel at generosity, while that person may have an unusual ability to strike up spiritual conversations and bring people to Jesus. This unusual effectiveness is the sign of a spiritual gifting.

Look through the list of spiritual gifts you wrote down on the previous pages. Who do you know who exhibits unusual effectiveness in some of these gifts? Write their names next to the gift.

2. WE DISCOVER OUR SPIRITUAL GIFTS AS WE ACTIVELY PURSUE THOSE RESPONSIBILITIES.

You're not going to discover your spiritual gifts by simply making an inventory of gifts and then assigning some of them to yourself. Instead, you're going to discover your gifts by obeying God and listening to others' observations about where we are most effective for Him. For example, you won't know if you have the gift of hospitality until you've obeyed God in extending grace to others. You won't know if you have the gift of teaching until you've tried it.

The Spirit of God called out Paul and Barnabas, for example, to a special gifting of evangelism and directed the church to send them out into the nations as their ambassadors (Acts 13:1-3). But before that, they were actively evangelizing their neighbors in Antioch. It was out of this obedience that God called them to their special task.

What gifts have others observed and affirmed in your life? What circumstances led you to exercise those gifts?

3. A SPIRITUAL GIFT USUALLY REVEALS ITSELF IN THE CONFLUENCE OF WHAT WE ARE PASSIONATE ABOUT, WHAT WE'RE GOOD AT, AND THE AFFIRMATION OF OTHERS.

The circle labeled "ability" refers to what you are naturally good at, "affinity" to what you feel passionate about, and "affirmation" to ways in which people in your church have testified how God has used you. Where all three circles converge is typically the place of a spiritual gift.

Often, spiritual gifts coincide with natural abilities you already have. God takes a natural talent and "supercharges" it for His purposes. Evidently, Paul was a great thinker and leader *before* he became a Christian, having been selected to apprentice under the highly respected Jewish leader Gamaliel (Acts 22:3). His special calling as an apostle and teacher coincided with his natural abilities to think and lead and write. (There are exceptions, of course. Sometimes, God gives spiritual gifts that have little to do with natural abilities, in part to highlight that power in ministry comes from God, not from talented people.)

When you consider the three circles—ability, affinity, and affirmation—which spiritual gifts seem most evident in your life?

CLOSING PRAYER

Offer yourself and your abilities to God, and ask Him to strengthen your passion for the areas in which He wants you to serve.

Day 4
SERVING THE CHURCH
EPHESIANS 4:15-16

Identifying and exercising your spiritual gifts isn't something just between you and God; it's between you, God, and His people. The purpose of exercising your gifts is not for a mystical, spiritual experience with God's Spirit on your own. It's not only about feeling fulfilled as a Christian. It's about fulfilling your role in the larger body of Christ.

This is the reason why God has given us *different* gifts.

> ⁴ For as in one body we have many members, and the members
> do not all have the same function, ⁵ so we, though many, are
> one body in Christ, and individually members one of another.
> **ROMANS 12:4-5**

If receiving spiritual gifts were only for our personal benefit, then it wouldn't matter if God gave us all the same gift. But since God has granted us different gifts, we know that His purpose for them is church-directed.

Let's return to Ephesians 4, one of the primary passages where Paul lays out the different gifts God has given His people. When he writes about the purpose of the gifts, he returns again to the image of the church as a body:

> ¹⁵ Rather, speaking the truth in love, we are to grow up in
> every way into him who is the head, into Christ, ¹⁶ from whom
> the whole body, joined and held together by every joint with
> which it is equipped, when each part is working properly,
> makes the body grow so that it builds itself up in love.
> **EPHESIANS 4:15-16**

Paul uses the imagery of a body held together by its different parts and working together properly. According to verse 16, what is the result of every person doing his or her part?

What will be the result if the joints are out of place or the parts are not functioning properly?

The Spirit gives His gifts *to you* *for* His people. Don't get so excited about the gifts He has given to you that you forget who they are for—the building up of the church.

Imagine a scenario in which you are part of a team that is constructing a home. All the materials were divvied out at the start of construction. Different people have different responsibilities. One person is trained to handle the chainsaw. Another person is stacking two-by-fours and plywood. Someone is laying down a concrete foundation. Someone else has a pouch with hammers, nails, screws, and screwdrivers.

What if one of the team members was so enthralled with what they'd received that they went off to the side and used the materials for their own benefit? For example, the guy with the chainsaw starts sawing off branches of trees instead of cutting the wood for the new home. Or the person with the hammer and nails randomly targets two-by-fours regardless of where the nails are necessary. The home won't get built because the workers see the materials as for their own personal use and benefit and not for the construction process. They need to remember: *The materials have been given to them, but they're for the home.* Likewise, spiritual gifts are given to individual believers, but they're for the whole body of Christ, not just for you.

Below are several of the spiritual gifts mentioned in the New Testament. Record how each can be used to benefit the church.

Faith

Teaching

Discernment

Serving

Generosity

Mercy

What spiritual gifts have you exercised in the past for the benefit of the church?

CLOSING PRAYER

Ask the Spirit to guide you as you seek to fulfill your role in building up His people.

Day 5
SERVING THE WORLD
EXODUS 31:1-5

An often-overlooked dimension of the Spirit's guidance is how God uses our "secular vocations" as part of His plan for us in the world. We tend to reduce the Spirit's empowerment to church stuff, things like preaching, leading worship, or taking meals to shut-ins. And those are all great things.

Scripture, however, presents the Spirit at work also in our natural, "secular" giftings too, using them for His purposes in the world. These vocational abilities are not the same thing as the spiritual gifts, but they are still ways the Spirit works in and through us.

In fact, the very word *vocation* comes from the Latin word *voca*, which means "to call." Our vocational abilities are part of our calling. So if we want to know God's specific plan for us, we should think about "secular" skills, too.

List one or two skills you rely on in your everyday activities.

How does it impact your work when you consider that God has given you these skills for His purposes?

In Exodus 31, we find a brief description of two very important, although largely unknown, Old Testament characters named Bezalel and Oholiab. These two artists, one filled with the Spirit of God and another appointed by God as a helper, showed that fullness by the excellent way they made artistic designs, cut stones, and worked with wood.

> [1] The LORD said to Moses, [2] "See, I have called by name Bezalel
> the son of Uri, son of Hur, of the tribe of Judah, [3] and I have
> filled him with the Spirit of God, with ability and intelligence,
> with knowledge and all craftsmanship, [4] to devise artistic
> designs, to work in gold, silver, and bronze, [5] in cutting stones
> for setting, and in carving wood, to work in every craft.
> **EXODUS 31:1-5**

In this passage, the Spirit's presence is connected to several skills. List them below (from vv. 3-4).

Martin Luther observed that when the Lord answers our prayer "for daily bread," He does so in a variety of ways. He gives the farmer the skill and ability to plant the seed, and to grow and harvest the grain. He equips someone to build the road on which we transport the grain, and someone who will drive the vehicle that carries it. He equips the engineer who designs the plant that processes the grain, the store owner who packages the bread for purchase, and the advertiser who alerts us to its availability. Thus, God answers our prayer for daily bread by a multiplicity of vocational endowments.[3]

Discovering your vocational abilities is part of learning how the Spirit wants to use you on earth. The Spirit of God is in your work, just as He was with Bezalel and Oholiab, expressing His creative work of the tabernacle through them. The Spirit of God works through all of His people as they engage their abilities to arbitrate a case, build a wall, paint a picture, treat a body, or tweak an assembly line.

This means that not every person filled with God's Spirit goes into so-called "full-time ministry." Far from it! God may have included a number of "secular" skills in your design—such as dentistry, carpentry, accounting, or parenting. In stewarding those vocations and giftings, God cares for the world through you. So you can also get to know the Spirit's will for your life by getting to know the specific vocational abilities with which He has equipped you.

Stewarding our Spirit-given "vocations" means we must also think about God's larger purposes in a fallen world when we choose our vocations and where we pursue them. Our secular giftings can help us spread His gospel. So at our church we say, "Whatever you are good at, do it well for the glory of God"—and do it somewhere strategic for the mission of God.

How can God use your career or your skills to advance His mission?

CLOSING PRAYER

Thank God for the abilities and opportunities He has given you, and ask Him to help you steward them well for the advancement of His kingdom.

THE SPIRIT
SHEPHERD

"We thought God was calling us to adopt a child from overseas, but we've encountered some obstacles. God must not want us to adopt, after all."

"I'm not sure what direction to take. As soon as I get a perfect peace about it, I'll know what God's will is."

"All the doors are opening for me to take this job, but I'm waiting on God to show me what I should do."

The first statement above was made by a couple who assumed the presence of obstacles automatically canceled their initial sense of God's call. The second statement was from a senior in high school, trying to determine what college to go to and what career to pursue. The third statement was from an unemployed man who wanted to make sure that he was following Scripture when an opportunity availed itself.

In each of these cases, the individuals were looking for a certain coming together of "signs" that would show them the path forward. A smooth path, or a perfect peace, or an open door— they might be signs that you're moving in the right direction. But sometimes God's plan for you includes obstacles to overcome. Sometimes your hope for a "perfect peace" can paralyze you with indecision. And sometimes an open door is one you should close.

In this session, we are going to see how the Holy Spirit is our Shepherd. We've seen how one of the ways we can discern God's will is by taking a look at the gifts He has given us. This week, we will see how the Spirit of God shows us God's will in Scripture and leads us by His sovereign control of our circumstances.

WARM UP

DISCUSSION STARTER: We all make decisions every day. When big, life-changing decisions come our way, we consider all sorts of factors before making a choice.

What is one of the biggest decisions you have made?

What factors did you consider as you made the decision?

How did studying God's Word and considering your circumstances play into your decision-making process?

VIDEO TALKING POINTS

VIEW SESSION 5 on the DVD and use the following bullet points as a guide.

- God guides us through Scripture.

- What we need to do—the will of God—is found in the Word of God.

- Does God guides us through our circumstances?

- "Trust in the Lord with all your heart, and do not lean on your own understanding" (Prov. 3:5).

GROUP BIBLE STUDY
READ THE FOCAL PASSAGE: PROVERBS 3:1-8

DISCUSS THE CONTEXT

Proverbs 3:5-6 are well-known verses in the Bible. Once we place these verses within their context (as one part of instruction from Solomon), we see that trusting the Lord for direction is part of a life devoted to the cultivation of godly character.

Read verses 1-2. What role does Solomon expect his commands and instruction to play in the life of his son?

What do you think is the connection between "fear[ing] (revering) the LORD" and not being "wise in your own eyes"?

DISCUSS THE FOCAL VERSE

⁵ Trust in the LORD with all your heart, and do not lean on your own understanding. ⁶ In all your ways acknowledge him, and he will make straight your paths.
PROVERBS 3:5-6

When we are acknowledging the Lord in all our ways, He promises to work behind the scenes to "direct our paths."

What do you think it means for us to acknowledge God?

Much of the stress we feel about discerning God's will comes from assuming we are responsible for acknowledging Him and directing our paths. Why is it important for us to acknowledge God and trust Him to make straight our paths?

APPLY GOD'S WORD

Solomon instructs us to lean on God's willingness to guide us. How does it impact your decision-making to know that God wants to guide you, not keep you in the dark?

What are some ways that wise character leads to right decisions?

The Word of God is sufficient for guiding us in the ways of God. How does understanding this truth free us to make decisions based on wisdom we've gleaned from Scripture?

What should we do when we have no clear instruction from God?

How would you counsel someone who won't make a decision until experiencing perfect peace, finding a special verse from Scripture, or seeing an obvious open door?

CLOSING PRAYER

Consider closing your group session by summarizing the discussion and then by praying this prayer of Augustine of Hippo (A.D. 354-430) out loud as a group:

Grant us purity of heart and strength of purpose,
that no selfish passion may hinder us from knowing Your will,
and no weakness hinder us from doing it;
but that in Your light we may see light,
and in Your service find our perfect freedom;
through Jesus Christ our Lord.[1]

Day 1
THE SPIRIT-BREATHED BOOK
2 TIMOTHY 3:16-17

The most reliable guide to the will of God is the Word of God. God has given us His Word in order to reveal His will. *But how do I know what God wants me to do specifically?* you may wonder. The way you discern God's specific call on your life is by following God's general commands in Scripture. In this way, the Holy Spirit guides us to obey God's revealed commands, adopt His values, and become the kind of people He wants us to be—the kind of people who will know what He wants us to do. The apostle Paul pointed to the sufficiency of God's Word for guiding us in God's ways:

> 16 All Scripture is breathed out by God and profitable for teaching, for reproof, for correction, and for training in righteousness, 17 that the man of God may be complete, equipped for every good work.
> **2 TIMOTHY 3:16-17**

According to these verses, what is the origin of Scripture?

List the four things Paul says Scripture is "profitable for" (v. 16).

Looking back over your Christian life, write down how God has used each of these four things to equip you "for every good work" (v. 17).

The phrase in verse 17, "that the man of God may be complete," can also be translated "mature." What does it mean to be mature? Well, we know immaturity when we see it. The toddler who chooses to stick his finger in the wall outlet is in for a shock (literally)! It's a bad decision, of course, but it's because the toddler "doesn't know any better." Likewise, the teenager who hangs out with the wrong crowd, succumbs to peer pressure, and does something regrettable is being "immature." Their decision-making is not yet formed to the point where they can be trusted.

We often equate maturity with making wise decisions. And one of the reasons God has given us His Word is so that we can be shaped into the kind of people who make the choices His Spirit would have us make. Being made "complete" or "mature" means we are equipped for every good work. Surely "every good work" includes the big decisions of life, like where we are going to live and who we are going to marry. Though Scripture doesn't speak to these choices directly, it offers wisdom and guidance so that we can be confident in our decision-making.

> Describe a time you spent significant energy in thinking through a pressing decision. How did the wisdom you gleaned from Scripture help you through the process?

The Spirit who inspired Scripture is the Spirit who illuminates Scripture. He speaks through God's Word in order to make us wise. Reading Scripture isn't just a godly exercise in discovering information about Jesus. Rather, it is the Spirit's exercise in aiding our transformation, until we look more like Jesus.

> Do you think of reading Scripture as something you do for God? Or do you think of reading Scripture as allowing the Spirit to do something in you? What is the difference?

Along with Paul, the apostle Peter wrote that the knowledge of Christ (through the Bible) is the power for "all things that pertain to life and godliness" (2 Pet. 1:3). *All things* that pertain to life and godliness? That sounds much like Paul's promise that Scripture equips us "for every good work" (2 Tim. 3:17). Those are pretty tall promises!

But what else would we expect? The Holy Spirit shepherds us through the Word He inspired—the Word He continues to illuminate. We don't have to rely on incantations and random Bible readings, or the strange alignment of certain circumstances, or feelings we can't be sure are from God or the result of indigestion! God's Word is sufficient to train us in godliness, and through this Word, the Spirit makes us mature and sets us on the path of making wise decisions.

CLOSING PRAYER

Spend some time thanking the Lord for giving us His Word. Ask Him to use His Word to bring you to maturity and make you wise.

Day 2

GOD'S WILL IS HOLINESS
I THESSALONIANS 4:3; 5:16-18; EPHESIANS 5:15-18; ROMANS 12:1-2

When we say that God reveals His will to us through His Word, we are referring not to the specific decisions we are faced with, but with the life of holiness God intends for us, the kind of life that becomes the basis for making the right decisions. In other words, the Word of God is focused more on the type of people we should be and less on the specifics of what we *do*. When you become the kind of person God wants you to be, you will do what He wants you to do.

Nearly every time we find the phrase "the will of God" in the Bible, it refers to the shaping of our moral character. We are going to look briefly at four examples:

> [3] **For this is the will of God, your sanctification ...**
> **I THESSALONIANS 4:3**

Sanctification refers to our being "set apart" for God's purposes. We belong to God, and our holiness is to reflect His. God's will is that we be holy and set apart. So what are some specific actions that show we are God's sanctified people? Later in the same letter, Paul mentions a few:

> [16] **Rejoice always,** [17] **pray without ceasing,** [18] **give thanks in all circumstances; for this is the will of God in Christ Jesus for you.**
> **I THESSALONIANS 5:16-18**

Based on these verses, what are actions and attitudes that should characterize a believer's life, no matter the circumstances?

How does fulfilling God's will in these areas bolster our evangelistic witness?

Knowing that God's will for our lives is holiness, we can automatically rule out things that do not align with His will. We never have to ask, "Is it God's will that I marry an unbeliever?" Or, "Is it OK for me to live in constant fear and anxiety about the future?" Or, "Should I divorce my spouse if I'm unhappy in the relationship?" The will of God in these instances is spelled out clearly in Scripture. God doesn't want you to prayerfully consider what He has clearly commanded or forbidden. He wants you to obey.

But what about those areas in which we don't have clear commands? In another passage of Scripture, Paul contrasts foolishness with "understanding what the Lord's will is."

> [15] Look carefully then how you walk, not as unwise but as wise, [16] making the best use of the time, because the days are evil. [17] Therefore do not be foolish, but understand what the will of the Lord is. [18] And do not get drunk with wine, for that is debauchery, but be filled with the Spirit.
> **EPHESIANS 5:15-18**

What are the similarities between verses 15 and 17?

If it is the Lord's will that we be wise instead of foolish, how can we grow in wisdom?

In a similar passage, Paul calls for obedience and transformation, so that we will know what God expects of us:

> [1] I appeal to you therefore, brothers, by the mercies of God, to present your bodies as a living sacrifice, holy and acceptable to God, which is your spiritual worship. [2] Do not be conformed to this world, but be transformed by the renewal of your mind, that by testing you may discern what is the will of God, what is good and acceptable and perfect.
> **ROMANS 12:1-2**

CLOSING PRAYER

Ask God to renew your love for reading Scripture in order to better know the clear commands of God and grow in wisdom and maturity regarding decisions you are faced with.

Day 3
LEADING FROM BEHIND
PROVERBS 3:5-6

We've seen that Scripture is most concerned with the character traits out of which we make decisions, not the decisions themselves. God's Spirit speaks through God's Word in order to shape us into the people He has called us to be.

So how do we approach those decisions for which the Bible gives us no clear direction? Nothing in Scripture tells us whom exactly to marry, where to go to school, or how many kids to have. Does God leave us on our own in those decisions? No, He does not. Remember the proverb we studied earlier:

> ⁵ Trust in the LORD with all your heart, and do not lean on
> your own understanding. ⁶ In all your ways acknowledge
> him, and he will make straight your paths.
> **PROVERBS 3:5-6**

Authors Philip Jensen and Tony Payne helpfully distinguish between three kinds of decisions we make each day and how God's Word relates to each[2]:

I. MATTERS OF RIGHTEOUSNESS

These things involve a clearly revealed right and wrong in the Word of God; or, as it is called in Proverbs, "the path of folly" versus "the way of wisdom." It is never the will of God, for example, to cheat in your business, to put yourself in a compromising position where you are likely to feel tempted, or to use your money selfishly. God's Word clearly tells us not to do these things, and so there's no use even praying about whether to do them. The Spirit has already directed.

> Name three things you have considered doing that you know
> will never be God's will because they are forbidden in Scripture.

2. MATTERS OF GOOD JUDGMENT

In these kinds of decisions, we're not dealing with a particular commandment of God, but one decision *is* clearly wiser than another. King Solomon talks in Proverbs, for example, about how to go about choosing your circle of friends, a spouse, or even at what stage in life to build your house. God's Word may not have a specific "command" about who to marry, but godly wisdom gleaned from the Bible can still inform your choice.

> When have you or your family been faced with a decision where one choice was clearly wiser than another?

> What considerations or biblical principles helped you determine the wise course of action?

3. MATTERS OF TRIVIALITY

These issues involve matters of such little consequence that you shouldn't waste a great deal of time and energy on them. But you might wonder: *Can't small coincidences have massive effects? What if some small decision out of the will of God messes up my whole life?*

This kind of thinking paralyzes you with fear when making the smallest of choices. Some decisions are "trivial" and should be treated as such. God wants you to make what seems like the best choice and move on without fear. God remains in charge; nothing small or large will keep Him from providing for us or guiding us to the people and places He wants us to go.

The majority of God's guidance happens as the Good Shepherd guides us behind the scenes. God calls for us to pursue His will as expressed in His Word and to trust Him to guide in the details.

We don't have to obsess about various coincidences or every holy hunch. When God wants to give us special instruction in the application of His Word, He'll make it reasonably clear what He wants us to do, just as He did in Acts—for example, when the Spirit of God forbade Paul and Silas to carry the gospel into Asia, then specifically the province of Bithynia (Acts 16:7). Unless He breaks in with clear direction, we should follow the paths of godly wisdom, make the wisest decisions we can, and trust that God is guiding the whole process.

CLOSING PRAYER

Thank God for how He has "directed your paths" up to this point, working the details (large and small) according to His purposes. Ask Him to help you trust Him as you seek to obey His will.

Day 4
INTERPRETING OUR CIRCUMSTANCES
ESTHER 4:14

The Old Testament Book of Esther has a peculiar reputation in the Bible. It never mentions God. Yes, there's a colorful cast of characters, a dilemma of epic proportions, and a twist at the end that makes it one of the Bible's most dramatic reversals. But God's activity is "backstage," so to speak. To see His work, you have to read between the lines. And that's just what one of the primary characters in Esther's story did.

Mordecai, Queen Esther's relative and guardian, advised her to risk her life by appearing before her egomaniac, emotionally unstable husband and appealing for clemency on behalf of the Jews. His rationale?

> [14] Who knows whether you have not come to
> the kingdom for such a time as this?
> **ESTHER 4:14**

In other words, "It seems that God has put you in this place and at this time with this opportunity for this purpose." Mordecai seemed to discern what God wanted by reflecting on God's sovereign direction of her circumstances.

When have you sensed God giving you an opportunity or aligning your circumstances in such a way that you discerned the right direction?

Why is it important to have a deep confidence in God's sovereignty over your circumstances, whether good or bad?

At no point did either Esther or Mordecai get audible direction from God. Their story demonstrates that even when we don't see other signs of His activity, we can trust God continues to direct our circumstances. We are where we are for a reason.

Where has God placed you and what influence has He given you in your current stage and place in life? How are you seeking to fulfill God's call on your life during this stage?

We've all experienced times when we've misread our circumstances. Everything seems to be lining up a certain way, and then it all comes crashing down in a wave of disappointment. You felt like things were getting better when they suddenly took a turn for the worse. Or the job you felt like was God's next step in your career went to someone else. You had your life mapped out with a certain person, but she turned down your proposal. A sudden death in the family changed your entire view of the future. Trusting that God is sovereign is tough, especially when the circumstances seem to point in one direction and then suddenly shift. But let's not be surprised when we misread our circumstances. Or when He makes something good from our mistakes. Sometimes God fulfills His plans in ways that puzzle and perplex us.

For example, in Acts 8:1, the Holy Spirit scattered the existing church into the world through a severe persecution. It's doubtful any of the early Christians raised their hands and said, "Pick me! Pick me!" when it came to the persecution that scattered the believers. And yet these external forces that made the early Christians feel powerless were *God's way* of moving believers into the places God wanted them.

We need to hold our interpretations of our circumstances loosely. Yes, we can and should expect the Spirit to shepherd us through His sovereignty over the world. Paul often interpreted open doors as invitations by God to preach the gospel and closed doors as God's direction to go elsewhere. In 1 Corinthians 16:8-9, for example, he explained to the Corinthians that he would stay in Ephesus a little longer than planned because "a wide door for effective work has opened to me." No "Spirit voice"; just an open door.

But an open door doesn't necessarily mean it's God's will; nor does an obstacle mean it's not. Trust God to work in the opening and closing of doors, and continue to trust in the Spirit to put you where He wants you when He wants you there.

CLOSING PRAYER

Thank God for how He has directed your circumstances in the past, and ask for help in being open to the Spirit's direction in the future.

Day 5
LEANING ON THE SHEPHERD
PSALM 23

No one wants you to know God's will for your life more than God Himself. Until you recognize your utter dependence on God for direction and His benevolent heart toward you as His child, you won't seek Him when you make decisions, because either you think you don't need Him or you think He doesn't care enough to reveal the path to you.

Frequently throughout Scripture, God is portrayed as a Shepherd, and His people are portrayed as the sheep of His pasture. Such is the case in the well-known Psalm 23:

> [1] The LORD is my shepherd; I shall not want. [2] He makes me lie down in green pastures. He leads me beside still waters. [3] He restores my soul. He leads me in paths of righteousness for his name's sake. [4] Even though I walk through the valley of the shadow of death, I will fear no evil, for you are with me; your rod and your staff, they comfort me. [5] You prepare a table before me in the presence of my enemies; you anoint my head with oil; my cup overflows. [6] Surely goodness and mercy shall follow me all the days of my life, and I shall dwell in the house of the LORD forever.
> **PSALM 23:1-6**

Your idyllic picture of a sheep in quiet meadows gets shaken up when you realize being compared to a sheep isn't exactly a compliment. Sheep aren't endowed with a lot of innate wisdom and intelligence. They make one bad decision after another. They walk with their heads low to the ground. They have bad depth perception, so they don't see more than four or five feet ahead of them. If you leave them alone, you'll watch them walk headlong off of cliffs, drown in rivers, or fall down and become "cast" (unable to turn over off of their own backs, like a cockroach), the perfect position to become another animal's prey.

In God's mind, you're like a sheep. If a sheep is going to get to where it needs to be, it won't be because of its own sharpness and agility. It will arrive at its destination because of the competency and compassion of its shepherd.

In John 10, Jesus calls Himself the "good shepherd." What did Jesus do to demonstrate His goodness as the Shepherd?

Jesus spoke of knowing His sheep and His sheep knowing Him (John 10:14-15). Why is it important to be more focused on knowing God than simply knowing His will?

Being compared to a sheep may seem insulting at first. But perhaps we should take comfort in this analogy. Since the Shepherd who guides us is both competent and compassionate, and since He has promised to get us where we need to go, we can trust Him to guide us. Fulfilling God's will isn't up to our own abilities at discerning His plan and following Him; it's up to God's willingness to lead us.

We don't have to rely on our own ability to figure out God's will. We have to lean on the Shepherd's willingness to guide us.

What does stressing over "discovering God's will" communicate about our view of God as the Shepherd?

How does knowing that God can bring good even out of our "unwise decisions" free us from the need to obsess over every decision we face?

We can't fulfill the Great Commission apart from the Holy Spirit's guidance. The disciples knew that unless the Spirit guided them through this mission, they couldn't help but fail. They had no choice but to look to the Spirit for help.

Yet, even in this extreme dependence, they never reduced the Spirit's activity in their lives to some formula. They grounded themselves in the Word, obeyed Jesus' general commands, and looked to the Spirit to lead them—watching for Him, and assuming He was leading even if they couldn't see or feel Him. We must do no less.

CLOSING PRAYER

Pray Psalm 23, pausing after each line to express gratitude for the particular ways the Shepherd cares for and guides you as His sheep.

HEARING THE SPIRIT SPEAK

John was a businessman whose heart had begun beating for church planting.

Ever since a church planter had visited his church and cast a vision for a new church in a different city, John had felt a strong desire to assist him in the teaching responsibilities. The more he prayed, the more he knew the Lord wanted him and his family to move across the country and provide help.

From Scripture, John knew the importance of the Great Commission. In his personal time of prayer, he sensed this new calling on his life. But his wife, who was also passionate about church planting, didn't feel the same connection to the church planter or the city he would be planting in. Two of his closest church friends told him they were concerned about him moving his family when two of his children were teenagers. His pastor wasn't sure he had the gift of teaching, since he'd never really taught before. He advised him to exercise his teaching role in a more limited capacity at first, or consider supporting a church plant locally.

John wasn't sure what to do. Was the counsel he received from others an obstacle to overcome? A test to see if he would follow his heart no matter what others said? Or was the counsel God's way of redirecting his passion, helping him understand the nature of his calling?

In this session, we will see how the Holy Spirit speaks to us through His people (by means of wise counsel or specific insight) and in our spirit (by means of placing a burden on our hearts). We'll look at how the Spirit speaks in this manner and how we must judge all our feelings and counsel by the infallible Word of God.

WARM UP

DISCUSSION STARTER: Take a moment to discuss John's story described on the introductory page.

If you were John, what would you do in response to the counsel you received from fellow church members?

How do we judge between what we sense the Spirit is saying to us personally and our belief that the Spirit speaks to us through His people?

What advice would you give John?

VIDEO TALKING POINTS

VIEW SESSION 6 on the DVD and use the following bullet points as a guide.

- The Spirit speaks to us through His church.

- God speaks to us through our spirit.

- Hold your interpretation of everything except Scripture loosely.

- Never elevate anything you feel or say to the level of Scripture.

- Never elevate what someone says from the Holy Spirit to the level of Scripture.

- Don't eliminate the possibility that the Holy Spirit is moving and speaking.

GROUP BIBLE STUDY
READ THE FOCAL PASSAGE: ACTS 13:1-4

DISCUSS THE CONTEXT

The Holy Spirit appears 59 times in Acts, and in 36 of those appearances, we see Him speaking through someone. Empowering prophetic speech is the primary thing the Spirit does in Acts.

How do you think the men listed in verse 1 had come to be seen as "prophets and teachers"?

What role do you think worshiping the Lord and fasting played in helping these early believers become receptive to the Holy Spirit's voice?

Who "sent ... off" Barnabas and Saul in verse 3? Who "sent them out" in verse 4? What do these verses tell us about how the Holy Spirit works among and through His people?

DISCUSS THE FOCAL VERSE

> ² While they were worshiping the Lord and fasting, the Holy Spirit said, "Set apart for me Barnabas and Saul for the work to which I have called them."
> **ACTS 13:2**

The text does not specify how the Holy Spirit spoke to the early believers. How do you think they recognized His voice?

Have you found that the Spirit's calling on your life is general, with specific details coming into focus later, or specific from the beginning?

APPLY GOD'S WORD

Does the idea that God "speaks" to people make you nervous? Why or why not?

When have you sensed God speaking to you in a powerful and personal way?

How would you respond to someone who had a "word from the Lord" that was in contradiction to Scripture?

Have you ever said something to someone that God really used, even though you had no idea He was doing so? Or has God used someone's words in your life in that way?

In what ways can we better prepare ourselves to be used by the Spirit when we gather together with believers in worship?

CLOSING PRAYER

Consider closing your group session by summarizing the discussion and then by praying the words from this hymn by Charles Wesley out loud as a group:

Spirit, sent from God above, to teach His perfect will,
How I wait to learn Your love; I tremble and am still.
To Your guidance, I submit. All my soul to You I bow;
See me sitting at Your feet; Speak, Lord, I hear You now.[1]

Day 1

PROCLAIMING GOD'S WORD TO ONE ANOTHER
I CORINTHIANS 14:20-25

For many Christians, going to church is about gathering with other believers to sing a few songs and hear a nice sermon. And while gathering with believers, singing songs, and listening to a preacher *is* part of what it means to go to church, we must not reduce a worship service to the things *we* do. Whenever we make church about what we do, we miss what *God* wants to do for us through the service.

The point of gathering with other believers is that we seek to hear the Spirit's voice speaking through our brothers and sisters in Christ, and also, we seek to be used by the Spirit to speak truth into their lives. The point of hearing a sermon is not merely to learn what God has spoken in the Bible, but to hear Him speak *through* the sermon to us *individually*. So, attending a worship service is not primarily something we do for God; it's something God does for us.

Take a look at how Paul envisioned the early church gatherings. Pay attention to what he says here about prophecy (the act of proclaiming and applying God's Word to people in particular situations).

> 20 Brothers, do not be children in your thinking. Be infants in evil, but in your thinking be mature. 21 In the Law it is written, "By people of strange tongues and by the lips of foreigners will I speak to this people, and even then they will not listen to me, says the Lord."
> 22 Thus tongues are a sign not for believers but for unbelievers, while prophecy is a sign not for unbelievers but for believers.
> 23 If, therefore, the whole church comes together and all speak in tongues, and outsiders or unbelievers enter, will they not say that you are out of your minds? 24 But if all prophesy, and an unbeliever or outsider enters, he is convicted by all, he is called to account by all, 25 the secrets of his heart are disclosed, and so, falling on his face, he will worship God and declare that God is really among you.
> **I CORINTHIANS 14:20-25**

According to verses 24-25, what happens to an unbeliever as the result of Spirit-prompted prophetic speech?

Do you tend to see this Spirit-prompted speaking as exclusive to the pastors and church leaders? Or do you see it as something "all" believers are to do (v. 24)? Why?

Too many of us see church as something the leaders do on our behalf. We go, listen to the choir or praise team, and then passively sit and take in a sermon. But Paul's vision of the church is one where every member is proclaiming the Word of God to each other and testifying to the power of the gospel in their lives through the empowerment of the Spirit of God. We're all praising God (not just the worship leader), and we're all proclaiming His truth to one another (not just the preacher).

Hearing the Spirit of God speak to us the Word of God through the people of God ought to be our experience every time we gather. This can happen through the biblically-faithful songs, through the skillful exposition of God's Word, and through conversations with other believers where our sin is exposed, God's Word is explained, and our particular needs are addressed.

God still speaks. Gathering with the church isn't about the words we want to say to God. It's about listening to the Word He has given us. The Spirit of God fills the mouths of His congregation with His Word.

When have you felt like a sermon was speaking right to you?

When have you experienced God addressing you through another believer who was applying His Word to your situation?

CLOSING PRAYER

Ask God to give you a strong sense of anticipation to hear His voice the next time you gather with other believers. Ask Him to use you to speak truth into others' lives.

Day 2

RECEIVING COUNSEL FROM OTHER CHRISTIANS
I CORINTHIANS 12:7-8

The gift of prophetic speech takes two primary forms: preaching and words of wisdom and knowledge. In his first letter to the Corinthians, Paul explains how the utterance of wisdom and the utterance of knowledge are given to the church for the common good:

> ⁷ To each is given the manifestation of the Spirit for the common good.
> ⁸ For to one is given through the Spirit the utterance of wisdom, and
> to another the utterance of knowledge according to the same Spirit ...
> **I CORINTHIANS 12:7-8**

Paul never defines what the word of wisdom or word of knowledge is. Based on how God worked among His people in the Book of Acts, how would you define these two utterances?

Regarding the "utterance of wisdom," Paul was probably speaking about how God uses His church to speak wisdom into our lives, guiding us more fully into the paths of wisdom. Important decisions made in isolation often end in disaster. God guides us in the paths of wisdom by means of the church. Sometimes it is supernatural insights; sometimes it is just good advice and wise counsel.

Regarding the "utterance of knowledge," Paul was probably speaking of supernatural revelations about situations or people that believers have no way of knowing about on their own. Through a word of knowledge, God places information into the mouth of one of His children, giving specific insight into the secrets of an unbeliever's heart, which convinces the individual God is really present in the one speaking. The person realizes there is no way this person could know such things, apart from God revealing them.

It's important that we never confuse this kind of "prophetic revelation" with Scripture. This would be disastrous. Paul encouraged believers to "weigh" prophecies given by other believers (1 Cor. 14:29). In his first letter to the Thessalonians, he said, "Do not treat prophecies with contempt but test them all; hold on to what is good" (5:20-21, NIV). Paul would *never* say such a thing about the Scriptures.

In fact, God gave another spiritual gift complementary to the prophetic gift the discernment of spirits to help the church determine which things the Lord was saying and which He was not (1 Cor. 12:8-10). Application of the gift of discernment is never applied to the Scriptures themselves.

Scripture is in a class all by itself, but the Spirit of God is still moving and speaking in the church. His movements never contradict Scripture, nor do they add to its message. But the Spirit's presence in the church today guides His people in the application of His message and the execution of their mission.

Knowing that we are to exercise discernment in receiving counsel from other believers, why is it OK to be a little skeptical when someone claims to be speaking for God?

How can we "test" the prophecies, whether delivered through preaching, or through words of knowledge or wisdom?

When you gather with your church or your small group, do you do so with the expectation that God may have words—gospel promises, warnings, and exhortations—for you to give others in the church, or that He may have such words for others to give to you? Do you come ready to speak in the Spirit and listen for the Spirit? Paul instructed the believers in Corinth to come to church prepared to do just that. Paul envisions a gathering of believers in which many are given a word, or a hymn of praise, for others (1 Cor. 14:26). You see, God intends *all* of us to be His vessels in the church, not just pastors and leaders.

A New Testament "church service" consists of three things: the Word of God, the people of God, and the Spirit of God. The Spirit of God puts the Word of God in the hearts of the people of God. And when that happens, Paul says, believers are built up and even unbelievers recognize that God is alive and at work in His church.

CLOSING PRAYER

Ask God to give you a proper measure of openness and discernment as you listen to preaching, or receive words of knowledge and wisdom from other believers.

Day 3

GIVING COUNSEL TO OTHER CHRISTIANS
I CORINTHIANS 12:7-8

We've seen what it looks like when we receive counsel from other Christians, how we are to test prophecies in light of Scripture, and be both open and cautious to what the Spirit may say to us through other believers. But what does it look like for *us* to be the ones who speak truth to those around us? How can we be used by God to be the mouthpiece of His Spirit? If God is active and alive, speaking to and through His church, what happens when He wants to speak through you?

> When have you felt a strong desire to share a truth from God's Word with someone in a particular situation? How was your message received?

Whenever you sense the Spirit prompting you to share biblical truth or give counsel to another believer, you should make it clear you are not claiming the authority of God on your words, no matter how convinced you are that the Spirit might be speaking through you. Prophetic speech in our day never carries the authority or certainty of Scripture. So unless you have a verse reference to back up your words, don't say emphatically, "God says ..." Rather, say something like, "I believe God might have put this on my heart to say ..." or "As a brother or sister in Christ, can I share something with you?"

Words of prophecy should always be given with a lot of humility and a bit of tentativeness. Because, you see, when you claim the authority of God, you put the others in a terrible position; they must either fully heed your word or feel like they are rebelling against God. Or think you're a quack. Paul makes it clear that all prophecies are subject to "testing," including our own.

> Has anyone ever counseled you in a way that claimed God's authority over his or her words? How did you respond?

The best way to speak truth into someone else's life is by tying your words to actual Scripture. While you can't always be sure that what's in your heart is from God, you can be sure Scripture is. Often the Spirit of God places commands and promises from His Word in your heart to communicate to others. When you pass this on to others, you can be sure that what you are saying is from God, even if your timing is not!

> What specific verses of Scripture have you shared with other believers, whether to comfort, guide, or confront someone?

The gift of prophecy has a purpose: building up the church and guiding in mission. Therefore, you should only use it for those things. Paul says prophecy is for the "upbuilding and encouragement and consolation" of people (1 Cor. 14:3), and for guidance in mission. The ministry of the Holy Spirit is not given for personal empowerment or selfish gain. When you get the sense that someone is using "Spirit direction" to enrich their status or authority, you have a reason to be skeptical.

> What abuses of prophecy have you witnessed that make you hesitant to speak truth into the lives of others?

The gift of prophecy scares a lot of Christians, because they have seen how easily it can be abused in the church. We must be cautious, however, of throwing out the proverbial baby with the bath water and thereby discarding a gift God gave to His church for its good. The church in Acts depended on this gift for guidance in the mission. I don't think we have become so much more competent in our generation that we no longer need what they relied on so desperately! Are we less in need of the Spirit's guidance than those early Christians?

CLOSING PRAYER

Ask God to help you be open to His Spirit's prompting when He wants you to speak words of wisdom and knowledge to other believers.

Day 4
THE SPIRIT'S BURDEN
NEHEMIAH 2:12

Sit down sometime and talk to someone who is involved in a ministry upon which God has poured out blessing. Whether it's a woman who rallied a town to open a pregnancy support center, or a pastor whose church helped restore the core of an urban center, or a missionary family who has risked their lives to take the name of Jesus to unreached people, you'll soon discover that the spiritual fruit of their ministries began with a holy ambition that gripped their hearts.

> "I couldn't sleep anymore when I thought about the women in distress who needed our support."

> "I felt like God's heart was for the people in that part of the city, and ministry there was constantly on my heart."

> "I wept whenever I thought of generations of people who had never heard the good news of Jesus Christ."

The common thread in these stories is a deep impression from the Holy Spirit on the hearts of individuals open to God's guidance and willing to obey. As we are seeking the Lord through prayer, Bible study, and among other believers, we shouldn't be surprised that the burdens that are on God's heart come to rest on our hearts as well. We can see this phenomenon in Scripture. Take Nehemiah, for example:

> [12] Then I arose in the night, I and a few men with me. And I told no one what my God had put into my heart to do for Jerusalem. There was no animal with me but the one on which I rode.
> **NEHEMIAH 2:12**

Nehemiah wept when he heard of his countrymen and the ruined state of their beloved city. He sensed the call of God to assist in the rebuilding of Jerusalem's walls, and he believed God had put it into his heart. God didn't write His plan in the clouds in the sky; He meshed His own passion for Jerusalem with Nehemiah's spirit.

In the New Testament, we never see God *telling* Paul to go to Rome to preach the gospel. Yet, Acts 19:21 tells us that Paul "resolved in the spirit" to go to Rome. Apparently, Paul had a yearning to go to Rome that he perceived to be the impulse of the Spirit. Paul called it *his* "ambition" (Rom.15:20). Later, God directly affirms it through a vision (Acts 23:11), but it seems to have *begun* as a yearning in Paul. Paul redirected his whole life around it, calling it his life's "race" (Acts 20:24, NIV).

> When have you felt a particular burden in your spirit? Did you sense the Lord speaking to you by placing this burden on your heart?

In another place, Acts records *Paul's* spirit being "provoked within him" when he saw how thoroughly Athens had given itself to idols (Acts 17:16). He proceeded to preach one of the most famous sermons ever given, a spontaneous sermon that has become the basis for a lot of Christian apologetic approaches. Can anyone doubt that this provocation in Paul's spirit was actually the Holy Spirit? In saying that Paul did this because "*his* spirit was provoked within him," Luke did not mean to imply that this was Paul's work instead of the Holy Spirit's; rather, he meant that the Holy Spirit used Paul's own spirit to indicate to the apostle what God wanted him to do. The two spirits were united, after all!

Provocations in our own spirit are often provocations from God's Spirit. Because our spirit has been united to God's, unscrambling where ours stops and His begins can be difficult, if not impossible! When we let the Holy Spirit have His way in us, our emotions become melded to His.

> When has your spirit been "provoked" by a situation? How did this provocation change your plans?

We must not let what we feel in our spirit trump what Scripture says or the counsel we receive from other believers. We can easily mistake our own ambition for the leadership of the Spirit. But we should still be open to the Spirit's leadership in giving us a "holy discontent" about something, and His pointing to ways we can be involved in bringing about change.

CLOSING PRAYER

Ask God to so align your heart to His that you sense the weight of the ministry He wants you to be involved in.

Day 5
THE SPIRIT'S AMBITIONS
NEHEMIAH 2:12

Not every ambition in our heart comes from God, but God certainly uses holy, burning desires like these as a compass to point true north for our lives, to show us where He wants *us* to go, and how He wants *us* specifically to be involved in His mission. Do you have a "holy discontent" about something right now?

On a scale of 1 to 5 (with 1 being least and 5 being most), rate how disturbing the following situations are to you. Make sure you don't put a number beside each situation based on what you think should be most disturbing to you, but based on your current passion for making a difference in that area.

____ An unreached people group with no access to the gospel or a people group that is resistant to the gospel.
____ A ministry in your church that needs development.
____ A career field with little Christian influence or witness.
____ The suffering of the poor, the immigrant, the homeless, the minority, the addicted, the mentally ill, the sick, the grieving, the unemployed, the incarcerated, the widowed, the elderly, the hungry, or the ignored and the shunned.
____ The evils of injustice, corruption, sexual exploitation, ignorance, destruction, waste, and greed.
____ The millions of babies murdered each year in the name of freedom of choice and thousands of children orphaned or in foster care.
____ A school that is failing from lack of resources and parental support.
____ The many kids in your community growing up without knowledge of the Bible.
____ The broken, lost, or hurting among children, teens, singles, couples, families, or senior adults.

Consider the two or three situations you ranked as most personally disturbing to you. Might this not be God calling you to get involved in one or more of those things? You—and your church—are not called to be involved equally in *everything* on this list, but you will be called and empowered individually and as a body to tackle *certain* issues. Are you actively looking for those places where God is calling you to work?

> Why is it important to recognize that not every individual Christian is responsible to be equally involved in everything on this list?

> How can you assist and encourage other Christians whose specific passions and callings are different from yours?

Perhaps our "holy discontent" about something is not a lifelong calling, but our focus for where we are now. Sometimes God moves us to be involved in situations with particular zeal for a season.

> What ministries have you been involved with, only during a season of your life? What did you learn from your work during that time?

The whole mission belongs to the whole church, but God calls different churches and different individuals to *specialize* in particular aspects of the mission. There are two ways that Christians can misunderstand this important truth. The first misstep is when Christians think the part of the mission most important to them should be most important to everyone. They can become frustrated when other Christians are involved, not in their preferred projects, but in equally important aspects of ministry.

The second misstep is when Christians complain because their church is not doing enough in certain area. This is the Christian who complains that the children's ministry is not up to par, or that the church isn't doing enough in regard to orphan care, or that there isn't enough charitable activity in the community. These Christians criticize the deficiencies of their congregation without recognizing that perhaps God is calling them to get such ministry started, or to get involved in making a ministry better.

CLOSING PRAYER

Ask God to break your heart for the people and situations He wants you to focus your ministry on.

WHEN GOD SEEMS ABSENT

"My spirits were sunken so low that I could weep by the hour like a child, and yet I knew not what I wept for," wrote the great English preacher Charles Spurgeon about his experience of depression.[1]

Upon the death of his wife, Joy, C. S. Lewis cried out to God and described the response as "a door slammed in [my] face, and a sound of bolting and double bolting on the inside. After that, silence. You may as well turn away. The longer you wait, the more emphatic the silence will become."[2]

Stark words. Sad words. But these words also encourage us, because they show us that some of the Christians we most admire have traveled through valleys of sorrow where all they could hear were the echoes of their weeping. Valleys where the voice of God went quiet.

We've been discussing the ways the Spirit speaks and how we can have the appropriate posture of receptivity to listen to His voice. But what happens when you are at your most receptive and God seems to be farther away than ever? How do you walk through days where you are desperate and despondent to hear the voice of God, when you are looking for His light in the darkness, when you long for His presence, only to be met by the crushing silence of God's absence?

In this session, we will see that seasons of spiritual wilderness are not uncommon in the Christian life. Neither are they counterproductive. God's apparent silence is an important part of how He works in our lives and grows us up into the men and women of faith He wants us to be.

WARM UP

DISCUSSION STARTER: Looking back on his life and the suffering and affliction he went through, Charles Spurgeon said: "In itself pain will sanctify no man: it may even tend to wrap him up within himself and make him morose, peevish, selfish; but when God blesses it, then it will have a most salutary effect—a stippling, softening influence."[3]

> Do you agree with Spurgeon's statement about the need for God to bless pain? Why or why not?

> When has an experience of pain or suffering driven you farther from God?

> When has an experience of pain or suffering brought you closer to God?

VIDEO TALKING POINTS

VIEW SESSION 7 on the DVD and use the following bullet points as a guide.

- Feeling abandoned by God has been the experience of the greatest Christians throughout biblical history.

- Realize that feeling of abandonment is just an illusion.

- God does His best work in our darkest hours.

GROUP BIBLE STUDY
READ THE FOCAL PASSAGE: PSALM 88

DISCUSS THE CONTEXT

Psalm 88 is one of the darkest, seemingly hopeless psalms in the Bible. Aside from the first verse, there is no overt statement of faith in God's goodness and salvation. This psalm perfectly captures the experience of feeling far from and abandoned by God.

As you read this psalm, look for clues to help you discern what problems the psalmist faced (betrayal, pain, loneliness, etc.).

The psalmist appears to have abandoned all hope, and yet he is praying. How does praying help us through times of suffering, even when we feel like God has abandoned us?

The psalmist speaks of God as the One who is against Him. Yet, he also asks the Lord for mercy and help. Do you think the psalmist is right in attributing his sorrows to God? Why or why not?

DISCUSS THE FOCAL VERSE

13 But I, O LORD, cry to you; in the morning my prayer comes before you. 14 O LORD, why do you cast my soul away? Why do you hide your face from me?
PSALM 88:13-14

When have you experienced the feeling that God's face is hidden? Explain how it was difficult to walk with Him in faith during that time.

How does crying to the Lord, even when we feel He is absent, express a childlike faith in His promises?

Why is it sometimes necessary to walk by faith in God's promises alone, even when we can't see or feel anything?

APPLY GOD'S WORD

How do you counsel someone who says God "feels absent"?

Which characterizes your Christian experience more—sensing God's presence, or walking by faith without feeling?

In what ways has God used a painful trial or circumstance to shape you? What did you learn?

How does trusting that God is using our suffering for our good give us strength in our time of weakness?

In the garden of Gethsemane, Jesus faced loneliness and a sense of abandonment as He prepared to face the cross. How does knowing Jesus faced the full measure of our aloneness in our place help us see God as with us in the darkest hour?

CLOSING PRAYER

Psalm 88 may end in despair, but Psalm 89 picks up with a time of praise. Consider closing your group session by summarizing the discussion and then by praying the words from Psalm 89:1-8,52 out loud as a group.

Day 1
THE SILENCE OF GOD
ISAIAH 64:3-7

By His Spirit, God is alive and active in His church. Nevertheless, if you think that walking with Jesus means an endless series of miracles; burning bushes; still, small voices; warm fuzzies; and sensations of peace that pass all understanding, then you are going to be disappointed.

Many of the greatest (and most honest) saints have confessed that they had to walk through numerous valleys with *no* sense of God's presence, sometimes nearly going deaf from the heavenly silence. Such silence is particularly frightening after you've grown accustomed to hearing the voice of God or experiencing the Spirit's guidance. Consider the heartfelt plea of the prophet Isaiah, who contrasted the Lord's saving actions in the past with His apparent "hiddenness" in the present, due in this case to the people's sin:

> ³ When you did awesome things that we did not look for, you came down, the mountains quaked at your presence. ⁴ From of old no one has heard or perceived by the ear, no eye has seen a God besides you, who acts for those who wait for him. ⁵ You meet him who joyfully works righteousness, those who remember you in your ways. Behold, you were angry, and we sinned; in our sins we have been a long time, and shall we be saved? ⁶ We have all become like one who is unclean, and all our righteous deeds are like a polluted garment. We all fade like a leaf, and our iniquities, like the wind, take us away. ⁷ There is no one who calls upon your name, who rouses himself to take hold of you; for you have hidden your face from us, and have made us melt in the hand of our iniquities.
>
> **ISAIAH 64:3-7**

Based on the contrast of verses 5-7 to verses 3-4, what reason does Isaiah give for the Lord's silence toward His people?

How does the presence of sin affect our fellowship with God and ability to hear Him speak to us?

One of the reasons God may seem absent is because of the presence of our sin. When we choose to continue in sin rather than seek His presence, we cannot be surprised when He seems distant. We are, in effect, pushing Him away, and in this, we grieve His Spirit. Sensing that God is absent may sometimes be a result of our own harboring of sins.

> When have you tried to "hide" sin from God, only to discover that He then seemed "hidden" from you when you desired Him?

The silence of God is not always the result our sin. In fact, the experience of being in "the wilderness" spiritually is common for believers. When God calls someone to follow Him, He frequently sends them through times in the wilderness. Right after God first put into Moses a vision to see Israel led out of slavery, He exiled him into the wilderness for forty years to herd sheep. Or consider the story of David. After being anointed as future king of Israel by Samuel, what was David's next move? He went straight back to the pasture to tend the sheep.

> When have you experienced a "wilderness" in which God was preparing you for His work?

Jesus Himself was *driven by the Spirit* into the wilderness to be tempted (Mark 1:12), and this event took place right after His baptism, when the Father declared His pleasure in the Son. It's important to remember that the affirmation of God's love over His Son did not change from the Jordan River to the wilderness of temptation. Jesus' experience of these events was radically different, of course. He went from a spiritual mountaintop (with the Father's affirmation and the Spirit's presence upon Him) to a spiritual desert (where He was alone, famished, and tempted by Satan). But the same affirmation that God spoke over Jesus in the water was still true of Jesus in the desert. And the same affirmation that God gives you as His child—"You are My beloved!"—is true whether you are on the mountain or in the valley.

CLOSING PRAYER

Confess any sins you have allowed to affect your fellowship and experience of God. Ask for endurance whenever He next allows you to experience the wilderness.

Day 2
SANCTIFYING DARKNESS
ACTS 9:15-16

The conversion of Paul is one of the most dramatic turn-around stories in the New Testament. You have a man who went from village to village, rounding up Christians and throwing them in jail, and suddenly, after meeting the risen Jesus on the road to Damascus, he is going from village to village, seeking to *make* Christian converts. And *he* is the one who gets thrown in jail for his activities. God took a first-century terrorist and turned him into the greatest missionary the world has ever known! But Paul's mission work was not a triumphant journey of successes. Suffering was part of his calling. Take a look at what the Lord told Ananias, the man who was to meet Paul just after he encountered Jesus:

> 15 But the Lord said to him, "Go, for he is a chosen instrument of mine to carry my name before the Gentiles and kings and the children of Israel. 16 For I will show him how much he must suffer for the sake of my name."
> ### ACTS 9:15-16

What are the three categories of people who Paul would "carry" Jesus' name to (v. 15)?

How does the presence of suffering in verse 16 affect the way in which the mission of verse 15 will be carried out?

Paul would be the one to take the name of Jesus to Gentiles, Jews, and even kings. But none of this would happen apart from suffering. He was an emissary of a crucified King. How could he *not* face suffering if he were to represent the Suffering Servant who gave His life for the sins of humanity?

Darkness shouldn't surprise the Christian. After all, faith is best suited for the dark. If God wants us to "walk by faith, not by sight," then we shouldn't be surprised when we are called to press on when we can't see or feel Him (2 Cor. 5:7).

How does suffering "well" help us to represent Jesus well?

Martin Luther, who struggled with intense seasons of feeling like God had abandoned him, said:

> Faith in Christ is far from simple and easy because he is an astounding king, who, instead of defending his people, (apparently) deserts them. Whom he would save he must first make a despairing sinner. Whom he would make wise he must first turn into a fool. Whom he would make alive, he must first kill. Whom he would bring to honor, he must first bring to dishonor. He is a strange king who is nearest when he is (apparently) far.[4]

God sanctifies us by humbling us. He works His salvation out in us by taking us through the valley of the cross, which often means *feeling* alone and abandoned. That's why Paul had to learn to suffer (Acts 9:15; 2 Cor. 11:24-27). In reality, we most certainly are *not* alone during these dark times, but walking by faith means believing that we are not alone even when we can't feel the warmth of God's presence.

What aspects of suffering have been particularly humbling to you? How did these experiences shape you?

Another reason God often leads us through dark, silent valleys is that He wants to purify our hearts. *Why* do we want to be close to God? Is it because of what He gives us, or is it simply because we want *Him*? What is more valuable to us: God or His blessings? Sometimes God withholds *everything* from us except His promises in order to make us ask ourselves, "Is this—His promise—enough for me?" You can never know that Jesus is all that you *need*, you see, until He's all that you have.

So here is the all-important question, one that the survival of your faith in difficult times may depend upon: *Can you walk by faith in God's promises alone, even when you can't see or feel anything?* Can you delay gratification, even the gratification of "feeling" the Spirit? The just, Paul says, can only live by *faith*.

CLOSING PRAYER

Ask the Spirit to help you see dark times as part of His sanctifying work, both through His humbling you and purifying you. Ask for strength to represent Christ well when we go through times of suffering.

Day 3
WITH US IN THE DUNGEON
GENESIS 39

Transitioning from the spiritual mountaintop to the valley of darkness often happens so quickly that you feel disoriented by the change, like a jet-lagged drowsiness that accompanies you on a trip overseas, or the sense of vertigo that up is down and down is up. In the span of days or weeks, we can go from experiencing God in the most majestic and awe-inspiring ways possible to feeling like He has abandoned us.

Consider Elijah, the prophet of Israel whose famous showdown with the prophets of Ba'al on Mount Carmel brought down fire from heaven. Elijah experienced one of the most spectacular manifestations of God's power ever recorded. But just days later, we see him on the run from Queen Jezebel, depressed and despondent, afraid for his life and pleading for God to reveal Himself and His plan.

Consider David, the young shepherd boy who alone would challenge Goliath, the Philistine giant. David's successful battle ends with the cheers of his people. But the next years are spent on the run, hiding in caves as he seeks to evade capture by an envious King Saul. From the victory of the battlefield to the loneliness of the desert, David goes from mountain to valley.

> When have you gone from a spiritual mountain (with a deep and satisfying experience of God) to a spiritual valley (when it felt like God was absent)?

The stories of Elijah and David remind us that just because God *feels* absent doesn't mean that He actually is. Just because you can't track His footprints doesn't mean He's not walking beside you or holding you. Who thinks God abandoned Elijah, the great prophet? Or David, the king after God's own heart? As readers of their stories, we recognize God's presence, even when from their perspective, it seemed like God was missing. Furthermore, in Scripture we see that God often does His best work in our darkest hours. Perhaps the best example is Joseph. Here is one of Jacob's sons, the favored child who receives a multi-colored, richly ornamented coat. His envious brothers scheme to kill him, throw him into a pit, and then decide to sell him into slavery. Despite these horrible circumstances, the text tells us:

> ² The LORD was with Joseph, and he became a successful
> man, and he was in the house of his Egyptian master.
> **GENESIS 39:2**

Based on this verse alone, what was the result of the Lord's presence in the life of Joseph?

Perhaps Joseph saw his rise in the Egyptian household and knew from his success that the Lord was with him. But what happens next may have caused him to doubt God's plan. When Joseph refused the sexual advances from his master's wife, he was falsely accused of attempted rape. Then, the text tells us:

> ²⁰ And Joseph's master took him and put him into the prison, the
> place where the king's prisoners were confined, and he was there in
> prison. ²¹ But the LORD was with Joseph and showed him steadfast
> love and gave him favor in the sight of the keeper of the prison.
> **GENESIS 39:20-21**

From privileged state to prisoner status, Joseph's life had once again taken a turn for the worse. But even here, despite the terrible circumstances, "the LORD was with Joseph." Then again:

> ²³ The keeper of the prison paid no attention to anything
> that was in Joseph's charge, because the LORD was with
> him. And whatever he did, the LORD made it succeed.
> **GENESIS 39:23**

God was there, even in the betrayals and the darkness, and He was hard at work. Down in the dank well where his brothers had thrown him, Joseph learned that God saves even out of desperate circumstances. While a slave in Potiphar's house, he learned that God had equipped him to manage a large household. And in prison, Joseph learned the organizational skills he'd need to save a whole nation from starvation. Through it all, God worked in him the patience and compassion to forgive his brothers.

CLOSING PRAYER

Ask God to reassure you of His presence even when your circumstances make you feel alone.

Day 4
ALONE FOR YOU
ISAIAH 53:3-4

The beauty of the gospel is that, in the Person of Jesus Christ, God suffers *with* us, *instead of* us, and *for* us. Jesus suffered with us in that He took upon Himself our griefs and sorrows, bearing the full weight of our sin and all its consequences as He died on the cross. He suffered instead of us in that He bore the wrath of God toward sin, paying the penalty for our disobedience and rebellion. He suffered for us in that He conquered Satan, sin, and death through His sacrificial death.

Our Savior knows the sting of suffering and the feeling of loneliness. He was alone *with* us when He was in the garden of Gethsemane feeling abandoned by God. He was alone *instead of* us on the cross when He felt forsaken by God so that we could be accepted. He was alone *for* us, so that through His resurrection, He could win the victory and reconcile us to God forever.

> Which aspect of Christ's work on your behalf do you give most attention to: His suffering "with," "instead of," or "for" us?

> How does each aspect of Christ's work give us hope when we feel alone and abandoned by God?

The prophet Isaiah gave us a striking picture of the coming Messiah and how He would suffer:

> [3] He was despised and rejected by men; a man of sorrows,
> and acquainted with grief; and as one from whom men hide
> their faces he was despised, and we esteemed him not.
> [4] Surely he has borne our griefs and carried our sorrows; yet
> we esteemed him stricken, smitten by God, and afflicted.
> **ISAIAH 53:3-4**

At the cross, Jesus experienced the horror of rejection by His Heavenly Father: "My God, My God, why have You forsaken Me?" (Matt. 27:46, HCSB). It wasn't the pain of the nails that hurt Him most; it was the utter aloneness. And He did it so that you and I would never have to experience it.

Jesus faced our aloneness—the true abandonment we had brought upon ourselves through our sin—so that you and I would never have to. The Father turned His face away from His Son so that the Father would never have to turn His face away from us.

So when we feel abandoned—that's all it is, a feeling. A lying, deceptive feeling. It has to be. Jesus faced the full measure of our aloneness in our place and put it away forever. By His death, He reconciled us to God, so that we can know He will never leave us or forsake us. In some strange way we can never hope to comprehend, He was abandoned ... for us.

> Think of a time when you felt hurt, betrayed, or alone. How does it help to know Jesus felt those feelings in their fullness?

What do we do, then, when we *feel* alone? Simply: "walk by faith, not by sight" (2 Cor. 5:7). You must re-believe the gospel, that God has removed the full extent of the curse—all that could ever separate you from Him—and has given you Christ's complete righteousness in its place. You must re-believe that in His finished work you couldn't be closer to Him than you are right now, regardless of how you *feel*. And you must reclaim the promises of God, almost all of which are made to us for times in which God appears distant.

The gospel declares to us that God has made Himself close to us in Christ, holding us even tighter than a mother holds a newborn child (Isa. 49:15). When our feelings tell us that is not true, we must defy those feelings with faith in God's promise.

So when you can't "feel" God, be assured, He's there. The cross assures you that He is. He will never leave you nor forsake you. Nothing can ever separate you from His love. He has united Himself, through His Spirit, inextricably to you. And just as with David, Esther, Moses, Joseph, and Paul, the Holy Spirit is likely doing His best work in you in those dark times.

CLOSING PRAYER
Spend some time thanking God for Christ's facing aloneness on your behalf.

Day 5
FAITH WITHOUT FEELING
2 CORINTHIANS 5:7

What you "feel" is not always a good indicator of what really is.

People who survive getting overrun by a snow avalanche often lose all bearings as to which way is up, and often will try to dig themselves out in the wrong direction. That happens to us in a time of aloneness. We "feel" like we are not close to God, but that feeling is not telling us the truth. God's Word tells us what reality is, not our emotions.

Emotions come out of our belief system; they should not be the basis for it. Our emotions, you see, do not have minds. They cannot think for themselves. We have to think *for* them, *telling* them what is real. Feelings should be reoriented around God's reality, not our perception of reality around feelings. And the best presentation of reality is found in God's Word. So we must believe our way into our feelings, not feel our way into our beliefs.

What are the dangers of having a feeling-based understanding of your faith?

What are some practices you can engage in to help you "believe your way into your feelings"?

Many Christians go through long seasons in which they feel disconnected from God, doubting whether or not they are even saved. The solution is to train our feelings to follow faith in God's Word. Feeling should arise from faith, and faith is built upon fact. When we reverse that order, allowing feelings to determine faith and fact for us, spiritual disaster occurs.

Second Corinthians 5:7 tells us, "We walk by faith, not by sight." We walk by faith in what God has said, not by feelings because of what we see. Renewed faith in God's promises, not renewed feelings, is what will lift us out of the pit of despair.

How have you experienced God's Spirit helping you to walk by faith in the dark seasons of your life?

The two of us (J.D. and Trevin) have experienced dark spiritual seasons, even when we've been obedient to God's call. When J.D. was a missionary in Southeast Asia, he went through a period of time in which he saw no fruit, no conversions. Conflict plagued his team. His prayer times with God felt perfunctory at best, drudging at worst. A few missionaries he knew had been thrown into a prison close by. He regretted ever coming to the field. "Where is God? Where is His blessing? Was this call an illusion?" he asked himself. Looking back now, he sees how much God was teaching him during that time. God revealed how much more concerned he was about his "success" in ministry than about his faithfulness to the Lord.

During a fierce Romanian winter more than a decade ago, Trevin stepped out of a successful ministry that he had poured himself into since moving there a year and a half before. As that period of ministry came to an end, Trevin felt stripped of his identity. He wondered if he had misread God's call on his life and worried that his time was meaningless. Looking back now, he sees how God was stripping away the idol of ministry success. Trevin had begun to so closely identify himself with that ministry that he could not make sense of his relationship with God apart from it.

These are lessons we desperately needed to learn (and still need to re-learn!), but no sermon could have taught them to us. We had to walk through the dark valleys with Jesus, unsure at times if He were even there, before those hidden areas of unbelief could be brought to light and healed by Jesus. Looking back, we see now that we've come to know God more in the pastures, wildernesses, and valleys than we have on the mountaintops.

Does it help us endure difficult seasons to know that God is teaching us something through them? If so, how?

CLOSING PRAYER

Ask God to help you rightly interpret the lessons He has taught you through difficulty in the past, and to guide you to endure the difficulties you will face in the future.

GOD'S GREATEST GIFT

Matthew 13:58 might just be the saddest verse in the New Testament. Jesus *"did not do mighty works there because of their unbelief."*

Nazareth. Jesus' hometown. Of all the places that Jesus must have wanted to pour out His saving power, Nazareth had to have been among the greatest. Yet, He did *almost none* of His mighty works there—not because of His unwillingness, but because of *the people's unbelief.*

The statement about Nazareth holds up a mirror in front of our own hearts and leads us to ask the difficult question: *Could the same be said of our families, our churches, or our communities?* Do we truly believe that the Spirit of God wants to move in our midst, to rescue the lost and embolden the saved, to change our hearts and transform our cities? Do we believe the Spirit is both able and willing to pour out salvation and transformation upon us?

Though we are near the end of our journey through the Scriptural teaching about the ministry and power of the Holy Spirit, we pray it's really just the beginning.

We want Christians to know deeply and personally how the Spirit of God has taken up residence in their hearts, and then grow in their gratitude for the gospel. We want to see Christians who are surrendered to the Spirit, willing to sacrifice for the mission of God. We need believers who recognize how God has gifted them for the benefit of the church and the extension of His kingdom. We want to see Christians who heed the voice of the Spirit through God's Word, His sovereignty over circumstances, counsel from God's people, and the burdens God places on our hearts. And when God seems absent, we pray Christians walk by faith in the darkness, persisting in prayer for God to do mighty works in our midst, for the glory of His name and the good of His people.

WARM UP

DISCUSSION STARTER: As our time of study comes to a close, use this week's opening to review what your group has learned and experienced thus far.

Of the seven sessions we've worked through so far, which one has been the most eye-opening or challenging for you during this stage of your life?

What are some steps you plan to take in order to strengthen your reliance on and experience of the Spirit's power?

VIDEO TALKING POINTS

VIEW SESSION 8 on the DVD and use the following bullet points as a guide.

■ Characterizations of an awakening to the Holy Spirit:

1. Confession of sin. Nothing drives out the presence of the Holy Spirit like willful, unconfessed sin in the church.

2. Remember the gospel.

3. Intense prayer.

GROUP BIBLE STUDY
READ THE FOCAL PASSAGE: LUKE 11:9-13

DISCUSS THE CONTEXT

This passage is part of the section of Scripture we call "The Sermon on the Mount." Luke's version is the "Sermon on the Plain." In this sermon, Jesus lays out the generous heart of God toward His children.

How are the promises of verses 9-10 based on how the father is described in verses 11-12?

Jesus commands us to pray, not because of what we need, but because of what God is like. Does seeing God as a generous Father prompt us to pray? Why or why not?

What are the biggest obstacles you encounter in being consistent and persistent in prayer?

DISCUSS THE FOCAL VERSE

> [13] If you then, who are evil, know how to give good gifts to your children, how much more will the heavenly Father give the Holy Spirit to those who ask him!
> **LUKE 11:13**

Why do you think the Holy Spirit is described as a good gift?

APPLY GOD'S WORD

How can we grow in our understanding of God's goodness to us?

How central would you consider prayer to be to your life?

What are some ways we can train ourselves to regularly ask God to fill us with His Spirit and empower us for ministry?

A. W. Tozer once said, "If the Holy Spirit was withdrawn from the church today, 95 percent of what we do would go on and no one would know the difference. If the Holy Spirit had been withdrawn from the New Testament church, 95 percent of what they did would stop, and everybody would know the difference."[1]

Do you agree with Tozer's statement? Why or why not?

If the Holy Spirit were withdrawn from your church, how much of a difference do you think it would make?

Tim Keller defines *revival* as "the intensification of the normal operations of the Holy Spirit."[2]

What are some of the normal ways the Spirit works in and through us?

Why is it important to ask with extraordinary faith for God to do mighty works while pursuing ordinary avenues of ministry?

CLOSING PRAYER

Consider closing your group session by summarizing the discussion and then by praying for revival out loud as a group:

Father Almighty, We trust that You desire to send revival and spiritual awakening to Your people. We believe that You can revive and renew us. So we pray that a hunger for revival would consume Your people. ... We desire to see evangelistic zeal consume Your Church. We cry out with the psalmist: Please revive us again, that Your people may rejoice in You! Amen.[3]

Day 1
SHAMELESS DESPERATION
LUKE 11:5-8

In our group study this week, we saw how Jesus commanded His disciples to keep asking, seeking, and knocking because God is a generous Father who delights in giving good gifts to His children, and the greatest gift He gives is the Holy Spirit. Therefore, our prayers are rooted in God's promises.

But let's back up a little in this teaching of Jesus. He gave His disciples this promise in response to an earnest request to teach them to pray (Luke 11:1). Evidently, you see, Jesus' disciples had noticed that prayer was the source of His power. They didn't say, "Lord, teach us to do miracles" or "Lord, teach us how to preach." They said, "Teach us to pray."

In response, Jesus told a rather odd little story about a man who had unexpected visitors late one night:

> 5 And he said to them, "Which of you who has a friend will go to him at midnight and say to him, 'Friend, lend me three loaves, 6 for a friend of mine has arrived on a journey, and I have nothing to set before him'; 7 and he will answer from within, 'Do not bother me; the door is now shut, and my children are with me in bed. I cannot get up and give you anything'? 8 I tell you, though he will not get up and give him anything because he is his friend, yet because of his impudence he will rise and give him whatever he needs."
>
> **LUKE 11:5-8**

When have you been completely desperate for something? How did the situation bring you to a point of powerlessness, where you were desperate for someone else's help?

Knowing some of the historical and cultural context helps us understand this parable of Jesus. Because his late-night visitors were hungry, the man went over to a neighbor's house to borrow some loaves of bread. His friend was already in bed, asleep, because that's what normal people do at midnight, especially since people in those days went to bed when the sun went down (thus making midnight the actual middle of the night.) Furthermore, families slept together, so to oblige this request this man would have to wake up everyone in the house. And on top of all *that*, the man asked for three full loaves of bread, which was enough to feed a family of six for a week! In other words, *this importunate neighbor had made a ridiculously excessive request at a most inopportune time.*

According to verse 8, what is the reason Jesus gives for this neighbor's generosity in the middle of the night?

The neighbor hands over the loaves of bread, not because the man is his friend (in fact, after this event, he probably wasn't his friend!), but *because of his shameless audacity in asking.* Won't your Heavenly Father then, Jesus reasons, who *never* sleeps, and who loves you like precious children (not a begrudging neighbor!), give you *the one thing* you desperately need to do His work?

What keeps us from prayer is the failure to acknowledge our utter dependence on God's power. Like a child pretending to be an adult, we are likely to see ourselves as more mature and self-sufficient than we really are. It's only when our world comes crashing down, and we wind up recognizing our desperation for God to act, that we begin to pray as we always ought.

We might think that tragedy or difficulty makes us more dependent on God. Actually, tragedy or difficulty only reveals our dependence on God. A moment of desperation merely reveals the truth that we are *always* utterly dependent on God. If you want to learn to pray, you must learn to see how desperate you are apart from God. The mask of independence must come off, and the charade of self-sufficiency must end before you will speak to God with the shameless desperation of someone who knows that only He can provide the answer.

When have you been at your most desperate in praying to God?

CLOSING PRAYER

Ask God to strip away your sense of self-sufficiency so that you will pray with shameless desperation, recognizing your utter dependence on God.

Day 2
PERSISTENT DESPERATION
LUKE 18:1-8

Jesus' promise that God will answer those who ask, seek, and knock refers to persistence in prayer, a continual knocking on the door until someone comes. We trust in God to give us good gifts, the greatest gift being Himself in the Person of the Holy Spirit, and then we express that trust through prayer. Not just any type of prayer, but persistent asking. We must ask repeatedly until God opens heaven's door and pours out blessing upon us.

"But why?" you ask. "If it is God's will to give us good gifts, if it is God's will to give us His Spirit, then why does He not give His power or His gifts the *first* time we ask?" In other words, why does God tell us to keep asking, seeking, and knocking?

There's no easy answer to this question, but persistence in prayer is something that Jesus clearly teaches. Charles Spurgeon said that some of the best fruits on God's tree are on sturdy boughs that require more than one shake to get them. God gives some things only when we persist in asking. Ask, and then ask again.

We've seen the shameless desperation of the man who went to his neighbor at midnight. In another parable, Jesus taught a similar lesson by contrasting God to an unjust judge:

> ¹ And he told them a parable to the effect that they ought always to pray and not lose heart. ² He said, "In a certain city there was a judge who neither feared God nor respected man. ³ And there was a widow in that city who kept coming to him and saying, 'Give me justice against my adversary.' ⁴ For a while he refused, but afterward he said to himself, 'Though I neither fear God nor respect man, ⁵ yet because this widow keeps bothering me, I will give her justice, so that she will not beat me down by her continual coming.'" ⁶ And the Lord said, "Hear what the unrighteous judge says. ⁷ And will not God give justice to his elect, who cry to him day and night? Will he delay long over them? ⁸ I tell you, he will give justice to them speedily. Nevertheless, when the Son of Man comes, will he find faith on earth?"
>
> **LUKE 18:1-8**

In what ways is God different from the unjust judge?

In your own words, explain the point of this parable in a sentence or two.

The shock value of this parable comes from the way it compares God to a cranky, old, unjust judge. And the idea of "wearing God down" through persistent, incessant, even annoying, requests seems sacrilegious, doesn't it?

But the point is not to *compare* God to an unjust judge, but to *contrast* Him with one. If even an unrighteous, selfish judge will grant answers because of persistent asking, Jesus reasons, why wouldn't God, who cares about His children as a tender Father, give us that one thing we need (the power of the Holy Spirit) when we come to Him persistently?

What are three things you are most persistent in asking God for whenever you pray? What do you think God wants you to persist in praying for?

What if we aren't experiencing God's power in our communities, in our churches, or in our families—simply because we are not persistent in asking? When the early church was up against a wall, they retreated into prayer, all night if that's what it took. The prayers of the church in Acts were not routine maintenance "organ recital" prayers ("God, be with Aunt Betsy's spleen, and Uncle Gordon's kidneys," etc.). We rarely (if ever) hear them praying for their safety. They simply prayed for boldness *in the Holy Spirit* to be faithful witnesses (Acts 4:29-31), and God answered so dramatically that the room shook. And after being shaken by the Holy Spirit, the threats of their enemies no longer held them back—they went out to shake the world with the gospel (Acts 17:6). Just like Jesus had promised, when they needed help, the good Father didn't give them a spirit of fear; He gave them the Spirit of boldness. Don't miss the order: they prayed, the Spirit shook them, and then they shook the world.

How can we move from praying mostly about personal and family needs to praying for boldness and grace as we engage in God's mission?

CLOSING PRAYER

Thank God for His willingness to hear and answer our persistent prayers. Ask Him to help you pray beyond yourself and your needs, for His kingdom to be extended through you.

Day 3
TWO KINDS OF GOSPEL WORK
PSALM 126:4-6

The Holy Spirit works in both ordinary moments and extraordinary movements. As we pray for God to move in extraordinary ways in the future, we must not set aside or minimize the ordinary acts of obedience we are responsible for in the present. But neither must we let our focus on ordinary steps of obedience today temper our hearts' desire to see God flood the world tomorrow with His power and grace.

The writer of Psalm 126 expresses a heartfelt longing for God to awaken and revive His people—to do something inexplicable apart from the power of God.

> ⁴ Restore our fortunes, LORD, like streams in the Negev.
> ⁵ Those who sow with tears will reap with songs of joy.
> ⁶ Those who go out weeping, carrying seed to sow, will
> return with songs of joy, carrying sheaves with them.
> **PSALM 126:4-6, NIV**

Bible commentator Derek Kidner points out that in these three verses, the psalmist has identified two ways in which God works in the hearts of His people.[4] In verses 5-6, the writer talks about "sow[ing] in tears." Israel had many desert regions, and the psalmist is imagining soil so arid that seeds planted needed to be watered individually, with tears. Imagine how many hours of exhausting patience and excruciating labor that would take!

God often works this way through us in the world. We patiently plant the seeds of God's Word in the hearts of those around us, water them with our tears, and fertilize them with our faith. Disciple-making can be laborious, painstaking work. Some of the greatest missionaries in history labored faithfully for years with almost nothing to show for it! Sometimes, ministry is long, laborious, and costly.

Have you ever been involved in a ministry that was difficult and costly, to the point you could describe it as "sowing in tears"?

What can God teach us through the experience of planting seeds and following His call, even when we are not seeing the results we hoped for?

130

God works through countless believers "sowing in tears," plodding through life in daily obedience, faithfully following God even when the work is hard and the results seem few.

But God works another way, too. The psalmist says, "Restore ... like streams in the Negev" (NIV). The Negev was a desert-like region in Israel with little vegetation. Occasionally, however, torrential rains swept the plains, and streams overflowed the land. When the waters receded, it left a moist and supple soil over which greenery spread like a carpet.

The psalmist imagines God doing this among the hearts of His people. This is what happened in Nineveh after Jonah delivered God's message. God did more in a moment through a shoddy sermon than a thousand missionaries could have done in two generations.

When have you experienced the Spirit moving through you or your church?

What were the signs to you that the Spirit was moving in a special way?

It's not wrong to yearn for an outpouring of God's Spirit. We ought to long for God to work in mighty ways in our midst. But such a yearning did not negate the psalmist's responsibility to plant the seeds and patiently water them with tears. Instead, it gave him a hope that he refused to relinquish, a hope that God would again send His Spirit into His land, like a flood. We should never give up that hope for our day, either.

Martin Lloyd-Jones described the heart's desire for revival: "We throw ourselves upon the mercy of God. It is not so much an organized prayer emphasis as it is an act of desperation. And then, and only then, does the power of the Holy Spirit come flooding upon us and into us. And he does in a moment what incremental organization can hardly accomplish in half a century."[5]

CLOSING PRAYER

Ask God to show you how He is working through your patient, plodding efforts for His kingdom. Ask Him also to give you renewed energy in praying for Him to pour out His Spirit like the streams in the Negev.

Day 4
PREPARING FOR REVIVAL
ROMANS 12:2

Some Christians think of "revival" as a series of church services scheduled over a week or two. But a true revival is not something we can schedule, plan, or bring about on our own, and any revival we *could* conjure up wouldn't compare with a true outpouring of God's blessings on His people.

So, if we are praying for God to do mighty works in our midst, to restore us like the streams in the Negev, how can we begin to prepare for God to move in extraordinary ways? How can we, like Elijah, build an altar in anticipation of God sending fire from heaven?

Our task could be put this way: we ask for revival with extraordinary faith, and then we pursue the "ordinary" means of grace. But what are those "ordinary" means of grace that will prepare us for revival?

The first "ordinary" action is to repent of sin. Throughout history, repentance of sin has always accompanied revival. Unconfessed, secret, or willful sin deeply grieves the Holy Spirit of God, and where it is cherished, the Spirit will not be present. Nothing quenches the fire of the Holy Spirit faster than unconfessed sin (Eph. 4:30-32; 1 Thess. 5:19). Willful sin makes the presence of God imperceptible to us.

True revival is not noisy; at least, not at first. It usually begins in a hushed awe. Believers get convicted about sin and the seriousness of God's holiness. Weeping is heard before shouts.

> What are some unconfessed or willful sins for which you need to repent?

A second "ordinary" way of preparing for revival is to proclaim the gospel faithfully. God's means for removing the veil of unbelief and planting seeds of faith is the preached gospel. Sometimes, when a church is proclaiming the gospel and few are listening, we are tempted to "supplement" the gospel with lights, music, humor, or Christian celebrities. There is nothing wrong with those things in and of themselves, but they can't replace the centrality of the gospel. Anything that distracts us from the preached gospel cuts off our access to God's power. We might still have huge audiences, but that's different than experiencing God's power.

So, if we're in a season where the harvest simply is not coming, the *last thing* we should do is abandon the only thing that can produce faith. We must continue planting the seed of His Word, watering them with our tears, and yearning for the streams in the Negev. Look at how Martin Luther described his role in the Reformation: "I simply taught, preached, and wrote God's Word; otherwise I did nothing. And while I slept … the Word did everything."[6]

> Why is the faithful proclamation of the gospel the essential element of any revival?

A third way of preparing for revival is by saturating yourself in the gospel continually. Israel's periods of spiritual decline were characterized by a "spiritual forgetting" (Deut. 4:9; 8:14; Josh. 4:20-24), and God brought awakening by "renewing" His people in the stories of His mercy (Rom. 12:2). Israel did not need to learn new things about the gospel; rather, they needed to have new eyes for the things they already knew.

Awakening involves believers "remembering" the great grace and glory of God, and feeling the weightiness of these things all over again. *Personal* revival comes from taking yourself deeper into the gospel. As you "remember again" your salvation, you grow in grace (2 Pet. 1:4-9).

> Why is it important for us to "remember" our salvation?

A fourth way of preparing for revival is by consistent and persistent prayer, birthed from the recognition that apart from God, we "can do nothing" (John 15:5). If you want to see revival, pray, pray, pray, and then pray some more. James Fraser, long-time missionary to China, said, "I used to think that prayer should have the first place and teaching the second. I now feel it would be truer to give prayer the first, second, and third places and teaching the fourth."[7]

CLOSING PRAYER

Ask God to stir up in you a holy desire for revival as you repent of sin, share the gospel, renew your affections through the gospel, and pray persistently.

Day 5
THE ACTS OF THE HOLY SPIRIT THROUGH YOU
ZECHARIAH 4:6

The Book of Acts tells the mind-blowing story of how a group of under-qualified, mostly blue-collar workers filled with the Holy Spirit can turn the world upside down. We're still reeling today from that first Christian century.

New Testament scholars have pointed out that when later Christians gave a name to the Book of Acts, they probably chose the wrong title. Rather than "The Acts of the Apostles," many say it should probably be "The Acts of the Holy Spirit." They say this because even a quick read of Acts reveals that the Spirit of God is the primary actor. *He* guides; *He* speaks, and *He* moves; the disciples are simply trying to keep up.

At *their* best, they are conduits of this mighty, rushing wind. At their worst, they are obstructions. In fact, they seem to spend a lot of time in Acts arguing with the Spirit (see, for example, Acts 9:13-14; 10:14-16). He slowly drags them to victory despite their dullness. It becomes readily clear that the Spirit, not them, is the one accomplishing the mission Jesus gave in Acts 1:8.

If God gave us the Book of Acts as an example of believers who are filled with the Spirit's power, why not ask God to do God-sized things through us today? Why not ask God to do things through us that are impossible to explain apart from His power?

If everything you do is explainable by natural giftings, then at your funeral people will likely give you credit for your accomplishments. But if God does things through you that are "*impossible* with people," then at your funeral your friends are likely to give God the credit. The Spirit wants to glorify Jesus in your life, not you. Live today with your eulogy in mind, asking God to do through you what only He can get credit for.

We should want the summation of our lives, then, to be the words of Zechariah the prophet:

> ⁶ **Not by might, nor by power, but by my Spirit, says the LORD of hosts.**
> **ZECHARIAH 4:6**

Let's yearn for the Holy Spirit to write a story through us that only His power can explain. I don't want my friends to summarize my life as "The Acts of J.D. Greear," but "The Acts of the Holy Spirit ... through and around J.D. Greear." He's writing the story of Jesus' salvation project through me. And following it as it unfolds has become the great adventure of my life.

What part of the story is He telling through *you?*

We hope this study has helped you see that the Spirit of God is beckoning you to follow Him. Maybe He has been beckoning you for a while, but you have been unaware. I hope through these pages you have seen that throughout your life God has been pursuing, calling, preparing, and equipping you for His work.

The choice is now yours. He beckons you to follow Him into a world of possibilities, impossibilities, dangers, and adventures. Remember, He didn't call you because He needed you. He called you because He loves you, He wants you to know His wonder and be amazed by His glory, and He wants to manifest His power in you. He wants to give you the privilege of being used by Him in the greatest rescue mission in the universe. He's got a purpose for your life, you see, greater than you ever imagined.

What lies ahead for you is so amazing that, if He let you see it all at once, it would probably blow your mind. Think about it: the angels, who see God's face every day, long to look into what you have—intimacy with God through the blood of Jesus and the fullness of the Holy Spirit. The Spirit, Paul says, is given to us as only a "down payment" of God's future plans for you (2 Cor. 1:22)! "Christ *in* you," Paul says, "the hope of glory" (Col. 1:27).

CLOSING PRAYER

If you are a believer, the power that brought the worlds into existence and Christ back from the grave is inside of you, waiting to be released by a simple prayer: "Yes, Lord, I will follow."

END NOTES

WEEK 1

1. Adapted from A. W. Tozer, *The Pursuit of God* (Ventura, CA: Regal Books, 2013), 28.

WEEK 2

1. John Stott, *The Message of the Ephesians* (Downer's Grove, IL: InterVarsity Press, 1984), ii.
2. Clement of Rome, "Prayer of St. Clement of Rome."
3. Quoted in D. Martyn Lloyd-Jones, *Joy Unspeakable* (Wheaton, IL: Harold Shaw Publishers, 1984), 95–96.
4. Jonathan Edwards, "Personal Narrative." Quoted in C. Samuel Storms, *Signs of the Spirit: An Interpretation of Jonathan Edwards' Religious Affections* (Wheaton, IL.: Crossway, 2007), 195.

WEEK 3

1. Apollonius, "A Prayer of St. Apollonius."

WEEK 4

1. Adapted from "Letter IV: Communion with God" in *The Letters of John Newton* (Edinburgh: Banner of Truth Trust, 1960), 29.
2. Adapted from *A Theology for the Church*, 2nd edition (Nashville, TN: Broadman & Holman), 540.
3. Gene Edward Veith Jr. summarizes Luther's thought this way in *God at Work: Your Christian Vocation in All of Life* (Wheaton, Ill.: Crossway, 2002), 10. Veith references Luther's "Exposition of Psalm 147."

WEEK 5

1. Augustine of Hippo, "A Prayer of St. Augustine of Hippo."
2. I follow here the categories set out by Philip Jensen and Tony Payne in their *Guidance and the Voice of God* (Sydney: Matthias Media, 1997), 90–98.

WEEK 6

1. Charles Wesley, "He Shall Teach You All Things."

WEEK 7

1. C. H. Spurgeon, *Sermons Preached and Revised by the Rev. C. H. Spurgeon, Fifth Series* (New York, NY: Sheldon and Co., 1859), 214.
2. C. S. Lewis, *A Grief Observed* (San Francisco: HarperCollins, 1961), 17.
3. C. H. Spurgeon, *The Complete Works of Charles Spurgeon Vol. 27*. Google Books.
4. The words here are those of Roland Bainton, summarizing Luther's teaching, from his biography of Luther, *Here I Stand: A Life of Martin Luther* (Nashville, TN: Abingdon Press, 1977), 171.

WEEK 8

1. As quoted in *Jesus, Continued … Why the Spirit Beside You Is Better than Jesus Beside You* (Grand Rapids, MI: Zondervan, 2014), 205.
2. Timothy Keller, *Center Church* (Grand Rapids, MI: Zondervan, 2012), 54.
3. Adapted from the Tennessee Baptist Convention.
4. Derek Kidner, *Psalms 73–150: A Commentary* (Downers Grove, IL: InterVarsity, 1973), 440.
5. D. Martyn Lloyd-Jones, quoted in Collin Hansen, *A God-Sized Vision: Revival Stories that Stretch and Stir* (Grand Rapids, MI: Zondervan, 2010), 15.
6. *Luther's Works, volume 51, Sermons I*, "Eight Sermons at Wittenberg, 1522," 77.
7. James O. Fraser, missionary to China, quoted in A. Scott Moreau, *Introducing World Missions: A Biblical, Historical and Practical Survey* (Grand Rapids: Baker Academics, 2009), 176.

TIPS FOR LEADING A GROUP

PRAYERFULLY PREPARE

Prepare for each group session by:

- reviewing the weekly material and group questions ahead of time;
- praying for each person in the group.

Ask the Holy Spirit to work through you and the group discussion as you help others take steps toward Jesus each week.

MINIMIZE DISTRACTIONS

Create a comfortable environment. If group members are uncomfortable, they'll be distracted and therefore not engaged in the group time. Plan ahead by taking into consideration:

- seating;
- temperature;
- lighting;
- food or drink;
- surrounding noise;
- general cleanliness (put pets away if meeting in a home).

At best, thoughtfulness and hospitality show guests and group members they're welcome and valued in whatever environment you choose to gather. At worst, people may never notice your effort, but they're also not distracted. Do everything in your ability to help people focus on what's most important: connecting with God, with the Bible, and with others.

INCLUDE OTHERS

Your goal is to foster a community in which people are welcome just as they are but encouraged to grow spiritually. Always be aware of opportunities to:

- invite new people to join your group;
- include any people who visit the group.

An inexpensive way to make first-time guests feel welcome or to invite people to get involved is to give them their own copies of this Bible study book.

ENCOURAGE DISCUSSION

A good group has the following characteristics.

EVERYONE PARTICIPATES. Encourage everyone to ask questions, share responses, or read aloud. Encourage everyone to get the most from the individual content, but be sensitive about making people feel guilty or pressured if not completing it.

NO ONE DOMINATES—NOT EVEN THE LEADER. Be sure what you say takes up less than half of your discussion. Politely redirect discussion if anyone dominates. Nobody is rushed through questions. Don't feel as if a moment of silence is a bad thing. People often need time to think about their responses to questions they've just heard or to gain courage to share what God's stirring in their hearts.

INPUT IS AFFIRMED AND FOLLOWED UP. Make sure you point out something true or helpful in a response. Don't just move on. Build personal connections with follow-up questions, asking how other people have experienced similar things or how a truth has shaped their understanding of God and the verses you're studying. People are less likely to speak up if they fear that you don't actually want to hear their answers or that you're looking only for a certain answer.

GOD AND THE BIBLE ARE CENTRAL. Opinions and experiences can be helpful, but God has given us the truth. Trust the Bible to be the authority and God's Spirit to work in people's lives. You can't change anyone, but God can. Continually point people to the Bible and to next steps of faith.

KEEP CONNECTING

Think of ways to connect with group members during the week. Participation during the group session is always improved by time spent connecting with one another away from the session. Encourage group members with thoughts, commitments, or questions from the session by connecting through emails, texts, and social media.

When possible, build friendships by planning or spontaneously inviting group members to join you outside your regularly scheduled group time for meals, fun activities, and projects around your home, church, or community.

MORE FROM J.D. GREEAR

The Gospel Revolution

On a journey to greater understanding of the gospel, Pastor J.D. Greear ran through all the religious activities typically associated with a disciple's life: giving, adopting, missionality, preaching, and witnessing. Though disciplined and intentional in all aspects, only when J.D. "discovered" the gospel of Jesus Christ did everything change.

You may understand the gospel. But have you let it completely redefine your life? Through this discipleship experience, group members will come to understand how to let the gospel work in their hearts the way religion never has…or could. (8 sessions)

lifeway.com/gospelrevolution

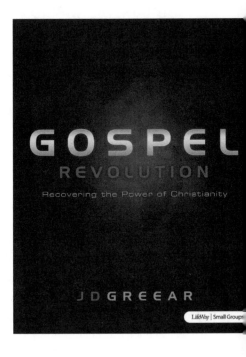

Ready to Launch

Christian parents are not seeking mere behavior modification in their children but the growth of truly godly passions. "Training a child up in the way he should go" must be done intentionally, with the mind and heart of God. Based on Psalm 127, this study plumbs the wisdom of the Bible about the goals of parenting, the stages of discipline, the role of the church, and strategies to shape the heart toward the gospel. (7 sessions)

lifeway.com/readytolaunch

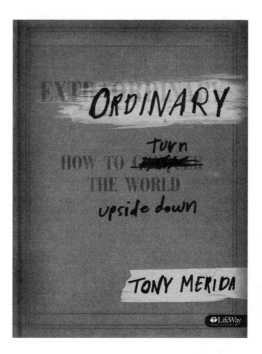
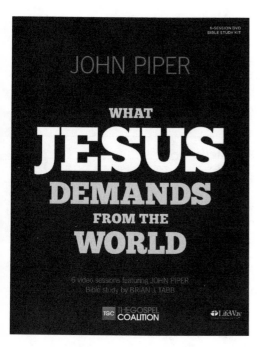

GROUP DIRECTORY

Name: _____

Home Phone: _____

Mobile Phone: _____

Email: _____

Social Media: _____

Name: _____

Home Phone: _____

Mobile Phone: _____

Email: _____

Social Media: _____

Name: _____

Home Phone: _____

Mobile Phone: _____

Email: _____

Social Media: _____

Name: _____

Home Phone: _____

Mobile Phone: _____

Email: _____

Social Media: _____

Name: _____

Home Phone: _____

Mobile Phone: _____

Email: _____

Social Media: _____

Name: _____

Home Phone: _____

Mobile Phone: _____

Email: _____

Social Media: _____

Name: _____

Home Phone: _____

Mobile Phone: _____

Email: _____

Social Media: _____

Name: _____

Home Phone: _____

Mobile Phone: _____

Email: _____

Social Media: _____

Name: _____

Home Phone: _____

Mobile Phone: _____

Email: _____

Social Media: _____

Name: _____

Home Phone: _____

Mobile Phone: _____

Email: _____

Social Media: _____